The Doubt
Illusion

The Doubt Illusion

A Compact Guide to Overcome OCD
with Inference-Based Cognitive
Behavioral Therapy

First Edition

Frederick Aardema, PhD

MR
MOUNT ROYAL
PUBLISHING

First Edition.

Cover design by Brian Halley.

Library and Archives Canada Cataloguing in Publication

Title: The doubt illusion : a compact guide to overcome OCD with inference-based cognitive behavioral therapy / Frederick Aardema, PhD.
Names: Aardema, Frederick, author
Description: First edition.
Identifiers: Canadiana (print) 20250291789 | Canadiana (ebook) 20250293781 | ISBN 9780987911995 (hardcover) | ISBN 9780987911988 (softcover) | ISBN 9781069796301 (Kindle)
Subjects: LCSH: Obsessive-compulsive disorder—Popular works. | LCSH: Obsessive-compulsive disorder—Treatment—Popular works. | LCSH: Cognitive therapy—Popular works. | LCGFT: Self-help publications.
Classification: LCC RC533 .A224 2025 | DDC 616.85/2270651—dc23

Dedication

In memory of my friend, Kieron —
philosopher, scientist, psychologist, researcher,
and also a mime artist, actor, and amateur magician.

The metaphors in these pages — illusion, theatre, and the tricks
of the mind — grew out of our many conversations about
imagination and the art of misdirection.

That spirit of creativity, insight, and playfulness continues to
shape this work.

Disclaimer

The information in this self-help book is not intended as a substitute for consultation with healthcare professionals, nor is it meant to diagnose or assess your individual situation. Neither author nor publisher warrants that the information contained in this book is in every respect accurate or complete and they bear no responsibility for any errors or omissions, or for any outcomes resulting from the use of the information presented herein. While this guide is designed to empower you, it may not fully address all your needs and is not intended to replace the expertise of a healthcare professional. If you experience any mental health concerns, you are advised to seek the help of a licensed mental health professional for assessment and treatment.

Contents

Introduction: Why This Book?

We all know doubt as a quiet companion — the nudge that makes us double-check if the stove is off or rethink a choice before committing. In its ordinary form, doubt keeps us careful, thoughtful, and safe.

But sometimes doubt stops being a companion and becomes a captor. It gets louder, relentless, and consuming. Instead of clarifying, it entangles.

You chase reassurance, but it never sticks. You reason, and the reasoning backfires.

What you're left with isn't ordinary doubt anymore. It's obsessional doubt — an expert illusionist that takes imagination and dresses it up as reality

What masks as an innocent question — *Did I lock the door? Did I say the wrong thing?* — is already part of the illusion. The thought doesn't simply appear and spiral; it enters on cue, after imagination has quietly prepared the stage.

If you've ever found yourself replaying conversations, second-guessing your motives, or stuck in the tug-of-war of *what ifs* that refuse to resolve, this book is for you.

Not because you need a diagnosis, but because doubt has begun to steal your peace, drain your energy, and crowd out the simplicity of living.

Traditional approaches to managing these doubts often advise us to "accept uncertainty" or simply "sit with distressing thoughts." Yet what if uncertainty itself isn't the issue? What if your mind is playing a trick on you — using flawed logic and vivid imagination to create doubts out of thin air?

That's where Inference-Based Cognitive Behavioral Therapy (ICBT) comes in — not as a new coping tool, but as a new lens.

ICBT treats obsessional doubt as a cognitive illusion — much like the act of a mime artist or magician. The performance may be convincing, complete with tension, drama, and perfect timing, but there's no real threat behind it. The illusion works because attention and imagination have been cleverly misdirected. Once you spot the sleight of mind, the effect dissolves.

ICBT is a scientifically validated, evidence-based treatment developed specifically for obsessive-compulsive doubt. Its effectiveness has been demonstrated in multiple research trials, and its principles are now applied worldwide by mental health professionals. This book distills those proven methods into a clear, conversational guide you can use in daily life.

Unlike traditional CBT models that often emphasize confronting fears or tolerating discomfort, ICBT focuses on how obsessional doubt is constructed — through imagination and reasoning errors that disconnect you from direct reality. Once you see this clearly, the fear begins to lose its hold. You don't have to white-knuckle your way through. You just have to recognize that the alarm was false all along.

This book is full of metaphors designed to give you the right key to break the illusion. ICBT is not a therapy of sheer effort or endurance — it's a therapy of realization and insight. Storytelling is part of that, because good metaphors change how you see.

The aim is not to expose *you* to OCD, as in some behavioral approaches, but to expose OCD itself — to the flame of reality. Not by dismissing imagination, or saying you're just "making things up," but by bringing imagination back into alignment with reality. OCD thrives on their misalignment. ICBT brings them back together — and that's where freedom begins.

This book draws from the same clinical foundation that informed the *Resolving OCD* series — the official guide and workbook written to give individuals and therapists a full therapeutic roadmap for applying ICBT in depth. Both projects were written in parallel over the past few years, designed to offer two distinct formats for overcoming obsessive-compulsive doubt: one comprehensive and structured, the other concise and conversational.

If *Resolving OCD* is a full-sized toolbox — heavy-duty, with every possible instrument you might need for a complete overhaul — *The Doubt Illusion* is the well-crafted pocketknife you carry in your pocket: light, simple, and built for everyday use. Think of it not as a shortcut, but as a different entry point — one that brings clarity through simplicity

Both tools serve the same goal — to free you from the grasp of obsessive doubt — but they meet you at different points on the journey. You don't always need the entire toolbox to fix the lock. Sometimes, all it takes is the right key.

This book isn't only for "milder cases." If you're struggling with severe OCD, you may still find relief here — either as a starting point or a companion to more in-depth work. It's for anyone who's ever felt stuck in their head — replaying thoughts, second-guessing choices, or overanalyzing moments that never resolve. If your mind often feels busy but never at peace, this book will help you see how obsessional reasoning keeps you trapped — and how to step out of it.

Across seven chapters, we'll gently unravel how obsessional doubt works — not by fighting every fear, but by exposing the process that made the fear feel real. Through vivid metaphors and real-world examples, you'll learn to stop wrestling with every *what if* and start walking right past them.

ICBT teaches a profound insight: your doubts often weren't grounded in reality to begin with. They were vivid, plausible, and emotionally gripping — but still just stories. And the more you learn to see them that way, the freer you become.

This guide won't just help you manage your doubts — it aims to free you from their pull completely. As you read on, you'll come to understand that obsessional doubt never represented a genuine problem to solve. It was, and always has been, just an illusion waiting to be unmasked.

Frederick Aardema, Ph.D., Clinical Psychologist
Full Professor, Department of Psychiatry and Addiction, University of Montreal
Clinical Researcher, Montreal Mental Health University Institute Research Center
Director, Obsessive-Compulsive Disorders Study Center
Montreal, August, 2025

Chapter 1
The Illusion of Doubt

The Illusionist in Your Mind

Imagine you're in a darkened theater. The crowd quiets, the lights dim, and an illusionist steps onto the stage. With a casual flick of his hand, the impossible happens: a coin vanishes. A woman floats. A locked box springs open.

You know it's a trick, but your stomach still tightens as if it were real. That is the power of a convincing illusion — even when part of you knows better, another part of you reacts like a believer.

Obsessional doubt works the same way — not a random storm of thoughts, but an illusionist in your head, staging acts that feel urgent and real.

One moment, life is normal. The next, a thought flashes across your mind: *What if I left the stove on? What if I insulted someone in that email?* Or worse: *What if I hurt someone? What if I'm secretly a bad person?* Before you know it, you're caught in the act, trying to untangle a mystery that doesn't even exist.

This illusionist doesn't have a single act — it's a shape-shifter. For some people, the trick is about safety — stoves, locks, germs. For others, it's about relationships, morality, or frightening scenarios that seem like warnings. The costumes change, but it's still a show.

At first, it feels like the mind is asking for answers — but it isn't. The questions are only part of the act. The more you engage, the more they multiply, as if the illusionist were changing tricks faster than you can follow.

Each "what if" feels like a search for truth, but it's really a performance meant to keep your attention on the show. And that's how the illusion deepens — the show pulls you in just enough to forget you're watching it.

You know, rationally, that nothing's wrong. You can look right at the stove and see it's off. You can remember apologizing for that harmless mistake. You can know from your values and lived experience that the fear doesn't match who you are — yet still the doubt whispers: But what if there's something you missed?

The illusionist inside your head is clever. It doesn't say, *This is definitely true.* It whispers, *But what if...?*

That tiny seed of possibility feels heavy enough to outweigh all the facts in front of you.

The more you try to fight these doubts, the worse they get. You check again, and again, hoping for relief. You replay conversations, trying to confirm you didn't say something offensive. Maybe you ask someone for reassurance. But the relief is like a cheap magic trick — quick, thin, and gone before you know it.

Within minutes, the *what if* returns, louder than before.

The real problem isn't the content of the doubt. It's never really about the stove, the door, the email, or the thought. The problem is the process — the way the mind quietly pieces together unrelated bits of information and starts treating them as signs of danger. Out of small, scattered hints, it builds the feeling that *something must be wrong*. That's what's called *inferential confusion* — just a fancy way of saying the mind mistakes imagination for evidence and ends up believing its own story.

It's like ignoring the clear sky outside because someone told you it *might be* raining somewhere.

Think of the illusionist again. When you watch a trick too closely, you get sucked in. You try to figure it out, but you're watching the wrong thing. The only way to break the illusion is to step back and realize it was never magic — only sleight of hand.

The same is true of obsessional doubt. It's not a sleight of hand, but a sleight of *mind*. You can't argue with it. You can't solve it.

You can only see it for what it is — a trick, a false alarm, a show that ends the moment you stop giving it attention.

What if you stopped trying to solve these doubts? What if you didn't treat them like urgent problems, but like stage tricks you could walk away from?

You don't argue with a magician on stage, demanding he explain how the coin vanished.

You simply accept it as a trick and move on.

This is what this book is about — not fighting your thoughts, not tolerating endless uncertainty, but recognizing the performance for what it is. Once you see the trick behind your doubts — the way imagination and reasoning stage a fake emergency — the lights come up. The audience vanishes. And what's left is quiet.

What Makes Obsessional Doubt Different?

We all doubt things. Doubt is normal. You might pause on your way out the door and wonder if you left the lights on. You check. The lights are off. Done. You might question if you paid that bill, so you check your bank app, see the transaction, and move on with your day. You might briefly wonder if you said something awkward during lunch, shrug, and forget about it.

That's how ordinary doubt works — quick, grounded, practical. It begins, finds its answer, and fades. Normal doubt is anchored in observation: you look, confirm, and move on. It's connected to the senses — to what's right in front of you.

Obsessional doubt doesn't work this way. It refuses to end — not because of missing facts, but because of the reasoning that built the illusion in the first place.

Something *might be* wrong, even when nothing shows it. The mind doesn't wait for uncertainty; it invents it. That subtle suspicion triggers a chain reaction. You can see the car locked, even remember locking it — and still your mind whispers: *What if you didn't really do it? What if it somehow unlocked itself?*

It doesn't stop there. Maybe the worry isn't about a stove or a door lock — it's about a thought, an image, or a fleeting feeling. You recall a moment and your mind suddenly intrudes: *What if this means something about me?* Imagination fills in the blanks — *What if I could harm someone I love?* Even though you know you never would, the mind turns the question inward: *What if I'm the kind of person who could?*

This is where the trick deepens. The illusionist in your head doesn't just tamper with what you see out there — it blurs your inner signals — your intentions, values, and sense of self. The quiet cues of your own mind begin to feel unreliable. A spark of irritation is mistaken for violent intent. A fleeting distraction in prayer is read as blasphemy. Forgetting a small detail gets twisted into proof of dishonesty. Even when your inner compass is clear, doubt acts as if it has uncovered some hidden darkness.

At that point, the doubt is no longer about the outside world — it's about you. The illusionist turns the spotlight inward, making you question your very character. What was once a flicker of imagination now feels like evidence of a hidden truth.

The fear of being negligent creates doubts about negligence; the fear of being immoral breeds doubts about morality; the fear of being unreal spawns doubts like *What if I'm not real?* or *What if nothing is real at all?*

That's what makes obsessional doubt so persuasive: it doesn't just question what you did — it plays on who you fear you might be.

That whisper doesn't care what you saw. It doesn't care what's real. It keeps asking for "certainty" while moving the goalposts so you can never give it enough proof.

You know your hands are clean after washing, but the thought nags: *Are you sure? What if you missed a spot? What if the germs are still there? What if they spread anyway?*

You can tell yourself you'd never cheat on your partner, yet your mind says, *What if you don't love them enough? What if the whole relationship is a lie?*

It's like arguing with a child who keeps asking, *But why? But how do you know? But what if...?*

The more you try to silence it, the louder it gets. You check again. You replay events in your head like a movie you hope will have a different ending this time. You go back to the sink, to the car, to the memory. You ask someone, *You saw me lock it, right?* And for a moment, you feel better.

Then the doubt returns, uninvited, smirking. It's like trying to stop an alarm clock by staring at it.

Normal doubt has one simple goal: find the truth and move on. Obsessional doubt is different. It doesn't have an end. It ignores the evidence, rolls its eyes at the facts, and refuses to shut up.

It's a hamster wheel.

It's not about finding an answer. It's about keeping you running, tiring you out while nothing actually changes.

Why is it so persistent? Because obsessional doubt is built on "maybe" thinking.

"Maybe" does not have an end. *Maybe I didn't check carefully enough. Maybe my memory is flawed. Maybe I missed something critical.* Or: *Maybe I'm fundamentally broken, fake, or unsafe to trust.*

There is always another angle. And unlike normal doubt, which trusts what your eyes, ears, and memory tell you, obsessional doubt throws all that out. It treats what's imagined as more relevant than what's experienced.

It even shows up out of context — a doubt about your health when you're just watching TV, or a violent image while you're peacefully chopping vegetables.

Everyday doubt matches the situation. Obsessional doubt barges in where it doesn't belong.

The illusion feels real not because of proof, but because imagination and fear fuse faster than you can notice.

The scene feels vivid, urgent, and real — so when the *what if* arrives, it doesn't feel like a question.

It feels like a warning.

The story doesn't wait for evidence; it creates its own. Your body reacts as if it were happening now — heart pounding, muscles tense, anxiety screaming that something must be done.

Even when a part of you knows the thought is absurd, another part whispers, *But what if it's true?*

That whisper feels heavier than logic. It feels like you must act.

And so you do: you check, you seek reassurance, you ruminate. But like a bad sequel, the thought always comes back.

The difference between normal and obsessional doubt is simple but profound. Normal doubt is tied to reality. It listens to evidence. Once the answer is clear, it leaves.

Obsessional doubt doesn't care about evidence. It's a false alarm — like a smoke detector tripped by stage smoke. No fire, just effects.

If you step back, common sense knows the difference immediately: if the door is locked, it's locked. If you have no urge to harm, then you are not dangerous.

The problem isn't that common sense failed you — it's that obsessional doubt talks louder, drowning it out.

The real problem isn't the imagined consequences — the fire, the guilt, the rejection — it's that the doubt appears at all, uninvited, built from imagination rather than observation.

That's the illusion. That's the show. And the sooner you see it, the sooner you can stop being its audience.

The Trap of Persistence

Normal doubt is like a question with an answer. Did I send the email? You check your outbox. Yes, there it is. Done. Did I lock the door? You glance back, see the bolt, and move on. Everyday doubts begin, get solved, and end.

Obsessional doubt, by contrast, never ends — because it was never asking a real question. It's performing a script. The mind mistakes imagination for evidence, then demands reassurance to confirm its own fiction.

It doesn't begin with a missing fact — it begins with a suspicion. And because suspicion has no endpoint, it never finds one.

You might be taking your nightly medication — a simple, routine act of care — and for a moment everything feels fine. Then, the thought intrudes: *What if you misread the label? What if you took the wrong dose? What if the pills got mixed up somehow?* You check the bottle, feel the cap twist tight, even recall hearing the click. Five minutes later, the doubt slides back in through a different crack.

Or it might not be about objects at all. Maybe you touched something and suddenly feel *mentally contaminated* — dirty on the inside, as though guilt or badness could spread through thought alone. Maybe you looked at someone and felt a flicker of warmth, and now the whisper says, *What if this means something about my sexuality? What if I'm not who I thought I was?* Or perhaps your reflection catches your eye and you wonder, *What if I'm not really me? What if I'm morphing into someone else?*

The cruel trick is that every attempt to fix the doubt feels like progress. You tell yourself, *I'll just check one more time. I'll think it through again. I'll be done once I'm sure.*

And for a moment, it works. Relief drifts in like a cool breeze —
brief, light, almost convincing. Then it slips away, leaving the
same unease behind, only stronger. Now you're right back where
you started, more tired, more uncertain, and more convinced that
the doubt must mean something.

It's the perfect trap: every effort feels like motion, but you're only
pacing in circles. Each check feels like movement, but nothing
changes.

It's like falling into a hole in the ground and deciding to dig your
way out. Each scoop feels like effort, like progress, but the walls
only rise higher around you. The deeper you dig, the further you
are from daylight.

This is why obsessional doubt is so exhausting. It creates the
illusion of solvability while refusing to be solved. You keep
feeding it answers, but answers are never what it wanted. The
doubt thrives on the chase itself. The more you reassure yourself,
the more it demands the next reassurance. Every time you argue
with logic, you're applauding the illusionist, keeping the show
alive. Each response becomes a new line in the script.

Take checking the door. You know you locked it, you even heard
the click. But the whisper says, *What if you only thought you
heard it? What if someone unlocked it after you left?* So you go
back. You lock it again. You walk away, relief in your chest. Then
the thought returns: *Are you absolutely sure?* Back you go,
another round in the loop.

Or think about the invisible kinds of checking — the mental
reviews. You replay a conversation again and again to confirm
you didn't say something offensive, only to find the memory blurs
with each replay. You scan your feelings to make sure you really
love your partner. You analyze your past to see if you ever crossed

a moral line. Each pass feels like investigation, but it's only a rehearsal for the next wave.

That's the persistence trap. Obsessional doubt never concludes, because it isn't built to conclude. It can't resolve because it never started with evidence in the first place. It started with a "maybe," and maybes never run out. *Maybe I left the iron on resting on a sleeve. Maybe the candle wick was still glowing beneath the wax. Maybe the tap was dripping after I walked away. Maybe that sound wasn't thunder at all, but something I caused.*

A maybe doesn't stop — it just multiplies. Normal doubt looks for closure. Obsessional doubt looks for fuel.

The tragedy is that the harder you try to end it, the more endless it becomes. You keep pulling at the knot, but the rope was never tied to anything real. And you keep digging, only to find you're carving your way deeper underground.

That's why obsessional doubt feels so heavy, so stubborn, so maddeningly unsolvable. It doesn't matter if you've gathered all the facts. It doesn't matter if common sense is on your side. The doubt keeps dragging you back for one more round, one more check, one more reassurance.

Every repetition sharpens the illusion — not the truth. It isn't just that the doubt doesn't stop. It's that you unknowingly teach it to come back stronger. The more you try solving it, the better the mind gets at rebuilding the loop.

And this applies to every theme — contamination, morality, safety, identity, existence. Each one borrows the same script: suspicion, checking, relief, return. The costumes change, but the act stays the same.

And the only way out is not to play along. Not to tug harder. Not to dig faster. But to pause, see the loop for what it is, and step out of it.

Why These Doubts Feel So Convincing

If obsessional doubt is only a trick of the mind, why does it feel so real? Because imagination has already done its work before the doubt even arrives. It doesn't whisper from the sidelines — it paints the scene in vivid detail and lets you step inside. By the time the thought surfaces — *What if something's wrong?* — the moment already feels charged with threat. The doubt doesn't create the story; it names what imagination has already built.

Before a single *what if*, imagination gathers details that seem plausible: the faint memory of once forgetting to turn off the stove, the smell of gas, a flash of smoke from a movie you saw years ago. When the doubt appears — *What if I left the stove on?* — it lands on a scene that's already burning. Your pulse races, your chest tightens, and your body reacts as though the fire were real.

It isn't that the doubt causes the reaction; the imagined reality came first.

It works the same way across every theme. A passing memory of a conversation becomes a full replay of your friend's disappointed face. A stray twinge of discomfort while driving morphs into a vivid image of having hit something. A neutral bodily sensation — a swallow, a breath, a blink — suddenly feels like a signal that something's off. A perfectly ordinary action or perception — a door closed, a light switched off, a sentence sent — becomes misread by imagination as unfinished or unsafe. The resulting tension is then labeled by doubt: *What if I didn't finish that properly? What if it's still not right?*

That's what makes obsessional doubt feel like a warning rather than a question. Your body reacts as if danger were present — not because it detected something real, but because imagination crafted a world convincing enough to fool your senses.

OCD doesn't invent new realities; it reshapes the one you're already in. It copies the signals of danger, guilt, or incompleteness so precisely that the illusion feels alive. The problem isn't that your feelings are wrong — it's that they're responding to a world that exists only in imagination.

This isn't about emotion overpowering logic; it's about imagination overpowering perception — the mind trusting what it built more than what it sees. The fiction doesn't feel true; it just feels real.

Here's the real sleight of mind: it's not that fear proves danger, or that emotion proves meaning. It's that imagination has made the unreal feel immediate. You're responding to a story that already replaced reality before the doubt began.

The way out isn't to argue with the feeling or find perfect logic. It's to recognize that the conviction itself was staged. The doubt was never evidence of danger — it was evidence of how powerful your imagination can be when it's turned against reality.

The Trick, Not the Content

The biggest shift you can make — the one that cracks the illusion wide open — is realizing that the problem is not the *content* of your doubts.

It's never really the stove. It's not the email. It's not the fear that jolted you awake last night. The real issue is the reasoning trick itself — the false move your mind makes before you even notice.

This is where so many people get stuck. They keep treating the doubt as if it's a real-life mystery to solve. You think, *If I just think it through again, if I replay the moment carefully, if I ask the right question, I'll finally feel certain.*

So you revisit last night's conversation. You replay your words, your tone, the look on the other person's face. Maybe you even text them to check if everything's okay — not because you truly believe you were rude, but because your mind insists the question must be answered.

Each attempt feels like progress — a scratch to the itch. But the itch didn't come from reality. It began the moment imagination replaced what's known with what's merely possible.

Trying to solve an obsessional doubt is like trying to reason with a magic trick. Imagine watching an illusionist pull a rabbit from an empty hat. You don't leap up and demand proof; you know it's sleight of hand. The trick works only when you're too absorbed to step back.

But when the illusionist lives inside your own head, spinning stories with your thoughts and feelings, it's much harder to step back. You forget it's sleight of mind and start treating it like life or death. Suddenly the rabbit feels real.

That's the key move: forgetting it's a performance.

OCD is a master of imitation. It doesn't invent new fears; it borrows what matters most — your morals, your safety, your relationships, your sense of who you are — and slips a false alarm among them.

The pattern is subtle but always the same.

First, imagination drifts from what is directly known into what might be — a "maybe" that feels personally relevant because it touches what you care about most: safety, morality, identity, control. That's where the confusion begins — abstract possibility starts to feel like concrete probability.

Next, the mind mistakes that imagined relevance for evidence — as if a feeling or a thought were a signal that something must be checked.

Then perception, reasoning, and emotion fuse — the mind's own sense of reality becomes convincing enough to feel like proof.

That is the essence of obsessional doubt: confusing abstract possibilities with relevant probabilities, and mistaking the mind's own sense of reality for proof. Once you see this, every *what if* reveals the same ingredients — not evidence, but imagination disguised as evidence.

Here's the truth: obsessional doubts are productions, not problems of reality. Stop treating them as emergencies and they collapse on their own.

What This Book Will Show You

When you start to see obsessional doubt for what it is — a trick rather than a real problem — everything begins to shift. The endless cycle of checking, analyzing, and second-guessing starts to look unnecessary, like arguing with a stage magician about where the rabbit came from.

The doubt was never asking for an answer; it was performing. And you, without realizing it, were sitting in the audience, applauding every move by reacting to it.

You don't have to outfight the illusion. You only have to stop taking the show seriously. Once you recognize that what feels urgent and life-or-death is mental sleight of mind, the spell breaks.

The way out isn't brute force or endurance — it's perspective.

This isn't a manual of rituals or mantras. It's a way of seeing. You'll learn to spot the move behind the illusion: how a "maybe" becomes a "must-check," how possibility dresses up as probability, and how that swap makes fiction feel real.

You'll notice how the performance pulls you off your senses — outer and inner — and how analyzing, checking, and replaying only tighten the loop. The fix isn't more proof. It's stepping out of the argument.

This isn't a book about "managing anxiety" or "accepting uncertainty." Obsessional doubt is not a real threat. It's not a puzzle to solve or a danger to prepare for. It's a mirage. Once you recognize that the oasis was just a trick of light, you don't need to convince yourself to stop walking toward it.

You simply stop.

The goal isn't control. It's freedom — the quiet freedom of realizing you were never actually stuck. Once you see that the performance in your mind is just that — a performance — you can step off the stage and back into your life.

Key Insights

- Obsessional doubt isn't a signal — it's a performance. The urgency you feel isn't truth knocking; it's a trick of the spotlight.

- Normal doubt checks reality and moves on. Obsessional doubt begins when the mind drifts from what's known into what's imagined and treats that as fact.

- The specific fear — stove, email, thought — doesn't matter. The illusion lies in *how* the doubt is made, not what it's about.

- Obsessional doubt hijacks both your outer senses (what you see, hear, remember) and your inner senses (what you know, think, feel, want, value).

- Imagination and faulty reasoning team up to create scenes that *feel* real but aren't. That's the sleight of mind.

- The persistence trap: the harder you try to dig your way out, the deeper you get. It feels futile — every check, replay, or reassurance barely touches the doubt, yet you can't stop doing it.

- You don't escape by solving the doubt. You step off the stage by seeing the trick and refusing to play along.

Try This: Everyday vs. Obsessional Doubt

Not all doubts play by the same rules. Some arise from reality itself — something concrete, observable, answerable — and fade once life settles them. Others begin in imagination — a *what if* that feels important but has no footing in what's directly known. Those are the ones that build a show.

The next time a doubt appears, pause and ask: Am I responding to something I can see, hear, or know right now — or to something I've imagined could be true?

If it's the second, you don't need to fight it or solve it. Just notice: *This is the illusionist performing again.*

That's enough for now. The trick isn't to solve the show — it's simply to remember you're in an audience, not on trial.

Chapter 2

The Stories Your Mind Weaves

How OCD Scripts the Scene Before Doubt Arrives

The curtain does not rise on a doubt. It rises on a drive home.

You're tired. You're distracted. The city slides past your windows like a film you've seen too many times.

At some point, you realize: *You don't remember the last few blocks.* The traffic light. The intersection. The pedestrian crossing. Nothing. Your memory's a blur.

Your mind leans in — not with panic, but with curiosity.

It starts assembling something.

A woman on the sidewalk — was she stepping off the curb? A flash of movement, maybe. No bump. No noise. But... something felt off.

Now your brain starts building a case. People cross without looking all the time. You once read about a driver who hit someone and didn't realize it until days later. That cyclist who darted in front of you last month — you almost didn't stop in time.

There are cameras on the street, you think. *If I did hit someone, it would already be online.*

You're not doubting yet. You're storytelling — sketching a plot before the doubt even arrives.

You're remembering news stories. You're replaying old near-misses. You're quoting your internal rules: *A good person would be sure. A responsible person wouldn't let this go.*

Each piece feels like a reason, a brick laid carefully in the foundation of a new story.

And then you remember that one strange look someone gave you as you passed.

That's when it lands: *What if I hit someone and didn't notice?*

Not as an idea. As a plot twist — the first sharp turn in a script your mind has been quietly drafting.

Suddenly, your ordinary drive home is part of a different production — one where you might be the villain and not even know it.

That's the power of your mind's narrative. It doesn't just drop thoughts into your head — it runs a film that casts you as both the protagonist and the potential threat.

It weaves facts, feelings, and fabrications into something that feels eerily believable—not by proving, but by stitching together just enough fragments to bridge the gap between what you saw and what you fear.

Most people think obsessive doubts come out of nowhere. But they don't.

They are built — with precision, imagination, and urgency.

That's the twist most people miss: before the doubt ever appears, the imagination has already written its script.

What Comes Before the Doubt

The doubts that keep you up at night don't fall from the sky. They don't sneak in randomly. They are crafted. Constructed. Built out of parts you already carry.

Maybe your story isn't about a car. Maybe it's about food, or faith, or relationships, or sexuality. Maybe it's about who you are, or what you might become.

Whatever the topic, the structure is the same: before the doubt arrives, your mind pulls from a library of fragments — facts, experiences, warnings, values, feelings — and starts to weave.

Some of these ingredients feel profound. Others are barely noticeable. Some feel obviously emotional. Others hide inside what seems like logic. But all of them share one thing: they pose as evidence, each adding weight to the case being built.

You remember abstract facts you've heard — that memory is unreliable, or that people can act without realizing it. These aren't false, but lifted out of context they stop being wisdom and become fuel.

Your mind promotes them to rules, background laws of the universe that justify worry, and suddenly you've crossed from perception into imagination.

You recall personal experiences. Past moments when you were wrong. When you forgot something. When you made a mistake.

These memories get pulled in not to inform you, but to accuse you — turning the past into a bridge that undermines the present.

Your values show up. Not as comforts, but as openings OCD can twist. Because you care about being kind, safe, or truthful, the doubt sneaks in disguised as loyalty to those values. It says, *If this really matters, you should treat this suspicion as serious.*

The values themselves are fine — it's the false story that leverages them.

You summon expert opinions — or what you remember of them. A therapist once said something about hidden intentions. A podcast mentioned false memories. A documentary showed someone who didn't know what they'd done until it was too late.

These borrowed authorities don't check the facts — they add credibility to the fiction. They're the "experts" quoted in OCD's courtroom drama.

You pull in stories from media. A scene in a show. A twist in a book. A headline. Even fiction becomes source material.

Your brain doesn't ask if it's real. It only asks if it fits the narrative arc already forming.

And then there's the feeling. A knot in your stomach. A sudden jolt of fear. A vague sense that something is wrong.

That feeling isn't the end of the story — it's the glue. It binds everything together. It turns loose fragments into urgency, the sense that this story isn't optional, it's critical.

Each element, on its own, might seem harmless. Even reasonable. But together, they form the scaffolding of the obsessional narrative. They create the bridge — carrying you from what you saw and knew into what you merely imagined.

They give the story its tone, its weight, its credibility.

And then the story delivers its payload. This is the central doubt — the hub around which everything else revolves. *What if I hit someone? What if I'm a bad person? What if I didn't really check?*

From there, the feared secondary consequences spin out — the headline on the news, the ruined friendship, the catastrophic fallout.

But those are just the movie's third act.

The engine of the story was already running long before the central doubt appeared — quietly assembling the plot that would make it feel inevitable.

When the doubt finally lands, it isn't random. It's the climax of a script that's been unfolding behind the scenes.

Why These Stories Feel So Convincing

Obsessional stories don't just stick because they're strange or scary. They stick because they feel *reasonable* — even intelligent.

They arrive disguised as ordinary thoughts, carrying the sense that they might make sense.

We tend to think the story forms after the doubt — that the mind gets scared first and then starts explaining why. But it's the other way around.

Below awareness, your mind is already assembling pieces of memory, logic, and emotion. By the time the doubt appears — *What if I missed something? What if I hurt someone?* — the groundwork is done.

You don't see the construction; you just feel the conclusion: *This could be true.*

Personal relevance gives the story its weight. It never wanders into random topics — it heads straight for what matters most: your kindness, your safety, your integrity.

The process feels rational. Everyday reasoning asks *What is?* Obsessional reasoning quietly slides into *What if...?*

It's imagination steering the wheel, but it wears the mask of logic. You don't think you're inventing — you think you're being careful, responsible, thorough.

That's why the stories feel *earned*. They sound like the voice of reason, but they're reason serving imagination.

And because the leap from faint suspicion to vivid scene happens in an instant, you rarely notice the scaffolding that made it possible.

Then emotion takes over. Even before the doubt is fully formed, the body reacts — a spike of adrenaline, a knot in the stomach, a flash of imagery so quick it feels remembered rather than imagined.

The story doesn't hand you proof; it hands you a feeling. And feelings are persuasive.

You know the stove is off, yet your chest tightens. Your heart races. The body whispers: *If I feel this way, there must be a reason.*

That layered construction — often unfolding in milliseconds — is what makes the fiction feel factual, and the doubt feel like a warning instead of a question.

The Bridge Between Reality and Doubt

Obsessional stories don't float in from nowhere. They need an anchor in something real — a scrap of perception, a faint memory, a flicker of feeling. But they don't stop there. They build a bridge.

You see the stove is off. Clear as day. But your mind whispers, *Knobs can malfunction.* Suddenly, the story stretches across that gap: from what you saw to what you fear.

You remember locking the door. You even recall the click. But your mind offers, *People sometimes imagine things.* The bridge is built, and now you're standing on the other side, wondering if you dreamed the whole thing.

Even feelings can be the anchor. A knot in your stomach becomes, *If I feel uneasy, maybe there's a reason.* And just like that, your body's signal is pulled into the plot, drafted into evidence for the case against you.

This is the hidden hand-off. A fragment of reasoning opens the door. Imagination rushes in and fills the gap with a scene. Then the body reacts — chest tight, stomach knotted — sealing the story as if it were fact.

It's like a relay race where the baton passes so fast you don't notice: reasoning starts the race, imagination carries it, and feeling crosses the finish line. By the time you catch up, the doubt already looks like it belongs on the podium.

The bridge always feels sturdier than it is. It borrows weight from facts, memories, or values — but the destination is fiction. You walk onto it trusting the first step, and suddenly you're in a world that looks convincing but isn't.

Once you see this move, it becomes easier to spot. You can notice: *Wait — I started with something real, but the story carried me somewhere unreal.*

That moment of recognition is the first crack in the illusion.

Because once you see the bridge, you don't have to cross it. And once you know the hidden hand-off is happening, you can stop treating it like proof and start seeing it for what it is — a trick.

The Illusion of Realism

What makes obsessional doubt so hard to shake is that it doesn't feel like a thought — it feels like an experience. You don't just wonder if something might be wrong. You feel it in your chest, in your gut, in the way your body tenses as though danger were already unfolding.

This is the illusion of realism — not realism as in truth, but realism as in immersive fiction. The kind that doesn't need to be accurate — only close enough to bypass your defenses.

Your eyes don't need to be convinced if your body already is.

A question like *What if I did something wrong?* never arrives as plain text. It comes with a quickening pulse, a shift in your whole internal landscape. The thought lands as though it were already halfway answered — already halfway true. And if it feels like a problem, your brain treats it like one.

Once you're inside that frame, the doubt is no longer an abstract possibility — it feels *present.* You stop being an observer and become a character in the story, reacting to events that never happened.

Obsessional doubt doesn't need airtight logic; it just needs plausibility. It puts you in the scene, hands you the script, and convinces you it's real life.

But fiction is what it is. Not revelation — performance. Feelings are persuasive, not proof. And the moment you remember that, the curtain lifts.

You don't have to fight the story. You only have to recognize it for what it is — words images, and sensations stitched into a show.

But what happens when you don't catch the trick in time?

What Comes After the Doubt

Once the story takes root, your mind doesn't let it sit quietly. It asks, *What would happen if this were true?* And then it answers — in vivid, emotional, high-definition detail.

You imagine pulling into your driveway, unpacking groceries, and later that night, a knock on the door. Police. Flashing lights. A voice saying someone was found injured, possibly on your route. They're just following up.

You picture yourself fumbling for answers, struggling to remember every moment of that drive. Your stomach drops. *Maybe there was a thud. Maybe you thought it was a pothole. Maybe you didn't check the mirror soon enough.*

Now your chest tightens. You feel anxious, dizzy. You scroll the news, just in case there's a report. You drive back along the same road, scanning for anything unusual. You replay your memory of the drive, over and over, like testimony you're rehearsing on a stage.

Was there a shadow near that intersection?

You ask someone — *Do you think I would know if I hit someone?*
You watch their face for hesitation.

This is no longer just a story. It's a *loop*.

The doubt you once believed was just a "thought" has grown legs.
It walks into every room with you. It hijacks your concentration,
your sleep, your ability to enjoy a meal or a movie or a
conversation.

You're on high alert, not because there's danger, but because
your body believes there might be.

Fear, then anxiety. And then, the compulsions: checking,
reviewing, confessing, Googling, avoiding. Whatever gives you
relief — even if only for a moment.

And here's the catch:

Every time you act on the doubt, you're not solving it. You're
feeding it.

You're telling your brain: *This is serious. Keep the story going.*
Your mind obliges. New doubts appear, new angles, new ways
this could all go wrong.

It spirals.

But here's the most important part: none of this would be
happening if the doubt hadn't occurred in the first place.

There is no spiral without the story that starts it. No anxiety
without the imagined consequence. No compulsion without the
illusion that something has gone terribly wrong.

And that's the irony. The focus on consequences is yet another
sleight of mind. It's like a magician setting a stage on fire to make

you stare at the flames, while the real trick happened earlier, hidden in the shadows.

OCD makes you chase the fallout — the imagined consequences and the feelings that follow — as if solving them could end the story. But that chase keeps the story alive. The real move happened long before. The obsessional doubt slipped in first, and once you were hooked, the rest was automatic.

That's why solving obsessional doubt doesn't start with managing anxiety or trying to resist compulsions. It starts further upstream — at the moment your mind builds the case. When it turns a flicker of *maybe* into a full-blown story, and casts you as both the villain and the hero.

It's not the consequences that drive OCD. They're just special effects. What drives the whole act is the construction of the doubt itself. The way it was made. The process, not the product.

And that's where we'll go next — into how these stories are built, why they're so persuasive, and how to see them for what they are before they pull you in.

Key Insights

- Obsessional doubt doesn't appear out of nowhere — it's the outcome of a story your mind has been quietly building.

- That story draws on real-seeming ingredients: facts, feelings, memories, values, authority — all woven into a compelling "maybe."

- The bridge from reality to doubt is built through a hidden hand-off — the mind takes a real perception or memory and quietly exchanges it for an imagined possibility.

- It doesn't feel like a hunch. It feels like a revelation. The narrative doesn't ask — it asserts.

- The emotional vividness of the story convinces you it must be true, even when no evidence supports it.

- OCD pulls another trick by fixing your attention on the feared consequences — the fire, the scandal, the confrontation— as if they're the real problem. But that's just misdirection. The real move happened earlier, when the doubt itself was constructed.

Try This: Catch the Prequel

The next time a doubt lands, don't wrestle with it. Instead, pause and ask: *What was happening just before this thought appeared?*

Was there a memory flashing by, a feeling in your stomach, a story you once heard, a value that matters to you? Often, doubts don't fall from the sky — they arrive with a prequel, stitched together from fragments of things you already know and care about.

You don't need to solve the doubt or disprove it. Just notice: *Oh — my mind built this story out of pieces.*

And if you want, as a playful reminder, take something ordinary — a sip of coffee, a walk down the street — and imagine it as the start of a story. Not because the story is true, but because it shows you how easily the mind can weave.

That's enough. The point isn't to edit or erase your thoughts, but to see them as stories — some worth keeping, others worth walking past.

Chapter 3
How to Build a Lie
(That Feels True)

Making the Illusion: An Overview

A good magician doesn't tell you they're about to trick you. They tell a story so engaging, so plausible, that you forget to watch for the sleight of hand.

That's exactly how obsessional doubt works. The trick isn't random. It's staged. The doubt is the grand reveal — but the setup has been happening in plain sight, one quiet step at a time.

In the last chapter, we watched OCD script the scene — pulling from memories, values, facts, and feelings until you're halfway inside a movie you didn't realize was fiction.

Now we step backstage. We're going to see how that story is built to feel real.

Think of a false confession. On paper, it makes no sense. Why would someone admit to something they didn't do?

Yet it happens — often — not because the person is guilty, but because the story they've been led into feels so convincing they start doubting their own reality. Memory gaps, pressure, imagined possibilities — and suddenly they're thinking, *Maybe I did.*

That's not evidence. That's perspective collapsing.

And that's what OCD's illusions do. You don't spiral because something true was uncovered. You spiral because your mind staged a scene so vividly that it felt like a hidden truth.

OCD doesn't barge into your day like an uninvited guest.

It builds its case slowly and cleverly, using the best parts of you — your logic, empathy, and self-awareness — and turning them against you.

The more you try to fact-check it, explain it away, or make it stop, the more solid it becomes — because every response is attention, like applause, more stage lighting that keeps the performance alive.

A magician makes something appear from nothing. OCD does the same — only instead of a rabbit out of a hat, it pulls danger from thin air and convinces you it was there all along.

The engine isn't fear. It's confusion — a subtle misfire in how your brain sorts the imagined from the perceived.

It's like mistaking a shadow for a burglar: the fear comes later, but the real error was treating the shadow as evidence in the first place.

OCD doesn't inflate the odds of disaster; it makes abstract *what ifs* feel personally relevant, right now.

You don't walk around braced for the ceiling to cave in, even though it's possible. But OCD takes that kind of distant possibility and reframes it as if it were knocking at your door.

This is how perspective collapses. What began as a faint possibility is elevated into a pressing probability — not because the world changed, but because your frame shifted.

The stage is reset, the spotlight moves, and suddenly the trick feels like truth.

And here's the key: it's not random. The illusion always unfolds in a sequence — three recurring moves that build on each other, followed by one final flourish.

In the sections ahead we'll examine each move in this mental magic act — the first thoughts that plants distrust, the story that expands it, the fragments of reality that get misused, and the moment you step fully inside the fiction.

Once you understand how the lie is made, you can start noticing the trap doors instead of falling through them.

The Con Artist's Tricks: How OCD Makes Fiction Feel Real

If OCD is the illusionist, this is its con artist's playbook—a carefully choreographed three-knockout-combo that takes you from certainty to collapse before you know you've stepped into the ring.

It never starts with the big reveal. It starts with a feint, a whisper, a small nudge. By the time the third punch lands, you're dazed enough to believe a lie with no evidence behind it.

It's not a clumsy scam. It's precise, patient, and staged like a con job or a magic act: one move opens the door, the next floods the room, and the last rearranges your own furniture so you think it's always been that way.

Each step is distinct, but together they build the same crescendo every time. This is why different OCD themes — health, relationships, morality, safety — all end up feeling eerily similar. The content changes, but the structure of the trick never does.

Trick One: Distrust of the Senses and Self
"It's Suspect!"

A great con never begins with the big lie. It starts by loosening your grip.

OCD does this by targeting what you rely on most—your senses, your memory, your self-knowledge.

You lock the door. You hear the click. You feel the handle secure. OCD whispers: *Did you really? Maybe you imagined it.*

You feel healthy, steady. No symptoms. OCD suggests: *What if something silent is already wrong—and you can't feel it yet?*

You remember being careful. OCD presses: *But can you really trust that memory?*

There's no evidence—only suggestion. Confidence erodes into that first hairline crack: *Maybe I missed something obvious.*

And once that crack opens, OCD wedges it wider with its signature tricks:

- Dismissing Inner and Outer Senses. You see the counter is spotless; OCD insists: *Your eyes miss things.* You hear yourself speak kindly; OCD asks: *Or was that just you imagining it?*

- Rejecting Common Sense and Self-Knowledge. You've always been careful. OCD reframes it: *Maybe you've secretly turned reckless and just haven't noticed.*

- Digging for Hidden Dangers. Truth must be "beneath the surface." *What if there's an undetectable illness? A hidden impulse? A buried confession?* The more you dig, the less ground you feel beneath you.

This is Hit #1 in the three-knockout-combo. Your knees wobble.

The dam that normally keeps imagination flowing calmly starts to crack.

And once it does, imagination rushes in.

Trick Two: Unchecked and Boundless Imagination
"It's Possible!"

Crack the dam and the river doesn't trickle—it floods. With trust weakened, imagination storms in, unanchored from direct evidence, spinning cinematic *what-ifs, maybes, might-bes,* and *could-bes* that feel more like memories than drafts.

- *What if I hit someone with my car?* You replay the drive, re-hearing bumps that never existed.

- *What if these thoughts mean I secretly want to harm someone?* A scene unspools so vividly it impersonates intent.

- *What if one careless moment caused a disaster?* Your mind storyboards the chain of catastrophe—frame by frame, consequence by consequence.

Your body salutes the movie as though it were happening now: heart racing, muscles braced, adrenaline surging. The soundtrack is loud enough to drown out common sense. Volume masquerades as validity.

OCD sharpens the blow with three imaginative distortions:

- Inflating Possibility into Urgency. A remote *maybe* becomes a pressing *now*. *What if that invisible thing in my body is already killing me?*

- Cinematic Mental Replays. High-definition internal movies of harm, contamination, or disaster—looped until they feel like recall. *You picture bleach fumes slipping under the door, filling every room until the whole house feels toxic.*

- Twisting Logic. *Careful people sometimes miss big things. I'm careful. So maybe I've missed something huge.* (That's not logic—it's costume jewelry dressed up as proof.)

This is Hit #2. With the dam gone, you're no longer standing beside a stream — you're swept into a flood.

Every imagined chord is louder than reason, until the mind feels carried away.

And then OCD makes another cunning move: it reaches back toward reality, not to free you, but to borrow its props.

Trick Three: Misapplied Reality and Artificial Relevance
"It's Real!"

This is the third hit—the one that drops you. After shaking your trust and drowning you in scenarios, OCD suddenly pulls you back toward reality—not to free you, but to *weaponize it.*

It grabs selective facts, familiar experiences, your own values—
and stitches them into the fiction until it feels like it has always
belonged in your life.

- You read a vague headline about sudden illness. OCD
  pounces: *That's exactly how yours will start.*

- You recall a tiny mistake from years ago. OCD reframes
  it: *Missed it once—you could be missing it right now.*

- You prize honesty. OCD weaponizes it: *If you were truly
  honest, you'd confess—even if you're not sure what
  happened.*

This is how the stamp of "real" gets forged:

- Cherry-Picked Facts. A stray article or out-of-context
  quote suddenly becomes *about you.*

- False Equivalencies. Someone else's slip becomes *proof*
  you're making the same mistake.

- Hijacked Values. Your best traits—care, conscience,
  honesty—are reframed as liabilities.

This is Hit #3. Distrust cracks the dam → imagination floods the
valley → misapplied reality stacks sandbags inside your living
room and calls it proof.

Normally, sandbags are meant to keep the flood out. Here, OCD
uses them to keep the flood *in*. It piles up fragments of fact,
memory, and value until the scene looks official.

The Result: A Lie That Feels Like Truth
(Without a Shred of Evidence)

And here's the knockout. The three-punch combo lands.

What started as a whisper of doubt now feels personal, urgent, and undeniable—yet it's built entirely without direct evidence.

This is OCD's real magic: a counterfeit world that looks and feels authentic.

You don't see blood on your windshield—yet every bump in the road feels like evidence of a hit-and-run.

You don't feel sick—yet every twinge or flutter is a countdown to catastrophe.

You don't remember cruelty—yet you replay every word you spoke, searching for the sharp edge you might have missed.

By now, you're not looking at reality anymore. You're watching the director's cut—a version of your life edited by doubt, spliced with ominous music, cropped to remove reassuring details.

It's like being accused of a crime with no fingerprints, no witnesses, no weapon—yet still finding yourself on trial, frantically defending against charges that don't exist.

From the outside, it looks absurd, even comical.

Who would second-guess a locked door after hearing the click? Who would fear illness with no symptoms? Who would cross-examine their own kindness?

But from the inside, it feels like responsibility. You're not chasing phantoms—you're being "diligent."

You think you're investigating clues, protecting others, preventing disaster. But really, you're trapped in a script your mind has been writing all along.

And just when you think the curtain has dropped, OCD is still backstage — set pieces ready, special effects primed — preparing its final, most immersive illusion.

The Final Flourish: Special Effects That Feel Like Evidence

OCD doesn't stop at suggestion, storyboards, and sandbags. It wants a standing ovation.

After the three-punch combo — distrust, imagination, and misapplied reality — it adds one last flourish: a masterstroke that flips cause and effect.

This is where the con turns immersive and experiential. It's no longer enough for OCD to tell you a frightening story. Now it has to sell you the experience.

Like a film crew adding smoke machines and sound effects, OCD rolls out sensations in your body, whispers in your head, and memories edited like reels of film — staged effects that feel like reality.

Phantom Experiences: When the Body Runs the Special Effects

Once doubt takes root, OCD shifts from storyteller to special-effects department. It produces sensations and emotions that mimic the very danger you fear, like fog machines and flashing lights that make a fake fire look real.

Think of it as a dress rehearsal. OCD tries the mask you fear most to see if it "fits," and the body obliges with effects convincing enough to pass as evidence.

These are phantom experiences—counterfeit evidence designed to pass for the real thing.

Picture someone afraid of contamination.

They walk through a public space, imagining germs clinging to their skin. Even without touching anything, their hands suddenly feel sticky.

Nothing's there—yet the sensation feels convincing enough to spark panic.

Or take someone doubting their relationship. In a tender moment with their partner, they suddenly feel emotionally flat. That flicker of numbness instantly mutates into "proof" they don't love enough—when in reality, the scrutiny itself snuffed the feeling.

These sensations aren't random glitches. They're the body's response to absorption. Anxiety dials everything up: breathing, heart rate, skin sensitivity, even the awareness of muscles you usually forget.

In another context, you'd shrug them off. Here, OCD filters them through the script of fear, and suddenly they're damning.

- Someone afraid of violence notices adrenaline in their arms and mistakes it for a dangerous urge.

- Someone fearing unwanted attraction registers a stray physiological flicker — tension, warmth, awareness — and mistakes it for forbidden desire.

- Someone terrified of choking notices their throat tighten—the more they monitor, the tighter it feels.

- Someone fearing illness feels their heart flutter and mistakes it for a symptom of disease — not realizing the flutter came from the fear itself.

- Someone trapped in existential doubt feels a sudden detachment, a brief sense that the world looks "off," and mistakes it for proof that reality has slipped away.

In each case, the sensation is a special effect — a reflex created by fear and attention, then misread as proof of danger.

What's experienced as "evidence" is really the body echoing the mind's imagined script.

Phantom Thoughts: Post-Production Confessions

But why stop at the body? If OCD can make you feel something that isn't happening, why not make you *think* something that never happened either?

This is Act II of the finale: phantom thoughts. They're the mental equivalent of CGI — computer-generated imagery, the digital tricks that make dragons fly or cities explode on screen.

If phantom sensations are the stage smoke, phantom thoughts are the costume fitting — trying on the very line you fear to test whether the mask will stick.

These aren't the original doubts. They're echoes that imagination adds later, crafted to make the story of fear feel complete.

Manufactured impressions. Lines delivered in your own mental voice. Images spliced into your memory reel — all designed to make the fiction feel undeniable.

Maybe it's a stray sentence that pops into your head, sounding like confession: *Do it now.*

Maybe it's a memory that suddenly looks different, edited overnight to appear sinister.

Maybe it's a vivid mental image that feels so sharp, you wonder if it's a hidden memory resurfacing.

The genius of this trick lies in its subtlety. These thoughts feel spontaneous and authentic — as if your deeper self is finally revealing the truth.

But they're not leaks from a hidden vault; they're special effects added in post-production. They appear *after* the doubt, but pretend to *precede* it.

The obsession generates them — and then the mind mistakes them as the source of the obsession. Examples:

- **Violent themes.**
  Doubt: *What if I'm secretly dangerous?*
  Phantom thought: *Do it now*, in your own voice.
  Trap: Mistaken for intent, when it's simply your mind running the scene you fear most.

- **Relationship doubts.**
  Doubt: *What if I don't love my partner?*
  Phantom thought: *You don't love them.*
  Trap: Mistaken for revelation, when it's really the echo of obsessive monitoring.

- **Sexual obsessions.**
  Doubt: *What if I have inappropriate sexual reactions?*
  Phantom thought: *A vivid sexual image.*
  Trap: Mistaken for desire, when it's your imagination simulating the scene.

- **Existential fears.**

  Doubt: *What if none of this is real?*

  Phantom thought: *You're the only real one here.*

  Trap: Mistaken for insight, when it's just your fear giving itself dialogue.

- **Moral or religious obsessions.**

  Doubt: *What if I m not a true believer?*

  Phantom thought: *A phrase or image that feels like a sin.*

  Trap: Mistaken for moral failure, when it's your conscience caught in OCD's echo chamber.

These are OCD's final special effects — the cinematic touches that make fiction feel self-evident. The thoughts and feelings don't confirm the story; they complete it.

And by the time they appear, the trick is already done. The illusion no longer needs proof — it *feels* true.

The Echo Chamber: When Effects Get Mistaken for Cause

Here's the masterstroke. The mind is a mimic.

When you expect a certain kind of thought, you often produce it— and then misinterpret it as discovery.

It's the moment the moviegoer forgets they're watching special effects and panics as if the explosions on screen are real.

OCD flips the sequence:

1. You generate the thought through focus.
2. You treat the thought as evidence.
3. You miss that the thought exists only *because* you were looking for it.

It's like staging a crime scene, planting fake evidence, and then "finding" it. You're not Sherlock Holmes here—you're both culprit and detective, dusting your own fingerprints and gasping when they match.

From inside the obsession, it feels seamless. You never notice yourself creating the thought, so it feels like it came from a hidden depth.

The whisper of *do it now* doesn't sound self-authored; it lands like a revelation — as if your mind has just exposed something dangerous about you.

That's why it's so persuasive: it feels like *input* when it's really *output*— a phantom line from the very story your fear scripted.

Think of it like shouting into a canyon. The echo bounces back and your body reacts as if something out there called to you.

But there's no voice in the dark—it's your own sound returning. That's the echo chamber effect: your fear ricochets, and when it comes back, you mistake it for proof.

And once the echo lands, the scene deepens. You stop being an observer of your thought and become a character inside them.

The special effects are so convincing you forget they were staged. The mind scripts a courtroom, a confession booth, a crime drama—and you're cast as both suspect and investigator.

That's the trick: you're not hearing a message from a hidden self. You're hearing your own echo — fear replayed as revelation.

The thoughts, images and sensations you experience aren't real; they're imagined, looping until they sound like you.

Special Effects That Fool Even Experts

And here's where the illusion gets its biggest assist from psychology's old story.

For years, OCD has been described as a problem of "intrusive thoughts" — random mental invaders that barge into your mind.

It sounds convincing because the effect *feels* real: these thoughts strike with force, as if hurled from the outside.

But that very sense of intrusion is part of the production.

OCD doesn't invade — it projects. It builds an echo, launches it into the canyon, and then gaslights you into believing something out there shouted first.

The traditional tale goes like this:

A random, disturbing thought pops into your head → you feel anxious → you try to neutralize it.

That story reassures people — and for good reason.

It helps to know that stray mental flashes are normal, that everyone has them, and that they say nothing about who you are. It's an explanation that takes the sting out of an odd or violent thought. It says: *You're not your thoughts.*

And that part is true.

But for OCD, that story stops short. It reassures, but it misses the real machinery — the hidden stagecraft that *creates* these so-called "intrusions" in the first place.

By the time the thought appears, the illusion is already mid-performance: imagination has set the scene, emotion has tuned the lighting, and attention has cued the line to hit with dramatic force.

These aren't random visitors — they're in-house productions. Phantom thoughts are *constructed*, not *inserted*: the mind rehearses the fear, then delivers its own echo as if it came from somewhere deep, dark, and true.

That's why they land so hard — not because they reveal something hidden, but because they were staged to feel revealing.

This is the real reversal.

The traditional model of OCD says:

Intrusive Thought → Fear → Obsession

But ICBT shows the true sequence:

Story → Obsessional Doubt → Echo → Phantom Thoughts

And that shift changes everything.

Because if you believe thoughts are random invaders, you grant them false authority — they feel like messages from the unconscious, warnings from your "real self."

In truth, they're props — special effects run by the same crew that staged your phantom sensations.

They feel profound because they arrive without effort. But effortlessness doesn't make them authentic — it only makes them look expertly produced.

So yes, these thoughts *feel* like intrusions. That's part of the con. OCD wants you to treat them as evidence — as whispers from within.

But when you see them for what they are — smoke machines, background noise, dialogue from a script you never meant to write — the illusion begins to break.

Living Inside the Lie: The OCD Matrix

If the tricks we've covered so far are the setup, this is the moment OCD ushers you through the door and bolts it shut.

Distrust has been planted. Possibilities have been spun. Fragments of reality have been twisted just enough to feel off.

Phantom sensations bloom. Phantom thoughts echo in perfect harmony with the story of fear. You're no longer watching the show from the seats — you're onstage under the lights.

It's like waking up inside *The Matrix* thinking you chose the red pill—the pill that promises a reveal, the sense that you're being pulled back toward clarity. You feel as if you've made a sensible choice – reality over illusion.

Yet the real switch happens here: that feeling of "seeing through" is itself a sleight of mind.

In truth, you were given the blue pill. You didn't return to the real world; you slipped deeper into a simulation that borrows the textures of reality well enough to fool you.

The scene isn't comforting; it's crafted to keep you inside the doubt.

Once you've crossed that threshold, absence of evidence no longer matters — the feeling now poses as fact.

Sensations, thoughts, and even memories are no longer neutral. They're suspects or star witnesses, depending on which role best serves the doubt.

The obsession no longer needs your full attention to keep going; it hums in the background, tinting everything you experience.

And here's the most disorienting part: from inside, nothing feels distorted. It feels obvious.

Like a vivid dream, the logic seems airtight while you're in it — only later, if you wake, does it reveal its absurdity.

Being in the bubble is not comfortable — it's suffocating.

But once you've accepted the doubt as real, leaving feels impossible. The world outside the bubble demands you trust yourself again, and from in here, that feels reckless.

So you remain trapped, not because you want to, but because every escape route looks like danger.

You keep engaging with the obsession — checking, solving, protecting — as if one more mental maneuver will finally restore certainty.

In reality, each action just tightens the snare:

- Scrubbing your hands raw after a faint stickiness that may never have existed.
- Replaying a conversation to catch the wrong tone in a sentence you can't clearly recall.
- Testing your emotions toward someone you love, waiting for the "right" reading that never comes.

It's like refreshing a frozen web page, convinced you're making progress while nothing changes.

The illusion remains intact, and OCD gets its encore.

Inside this simulation, the rules are simple — and impossible:

- If you feel it, it must be real.
- If you can imagine it, you must treat it as probable.
- If you can't remember perfectly, you can't trust yourself.

From the outside, these collapse instantly. From the inside, they feel like survival laws.

The longer you stay here, the more this altered version of reality becomes the only one that feels true.

A stranger's glance becomes a warning. A fleeting bodily sensation becomes a sign. A forgotten detail becomes a red flag.

OCD doesn't have to prove its story; it only has to keep you living in it until proof stops mattering.

And here's the cruelest sleight of hand: OCD makes you *feel* like you're being brought closer to the truth — like someone's offering you clarity — but what you're actually given is deeper entrapment.

The red-pill feeling is part of the stagecraft. It lulls you into thinking you're near clarity the illusion seals around you. You believe you're returning. You're not; you're further inside the performance.

It's here, in this sealed-off mental world, that OCD turns up the spotlight on its most personal trick — the one that's been threaded through the story all along.

From the very first doubt, it wasn't just about the door or the germs or the bump in the road. It was about you. That's the feared possible self, and that's where we'll go next.

The Feared Possible Self: The Lie That Feels Personal

By the time OCD's illusion is running at full strength, the doubt is no longer about an event or a possibility "out there."

It's about you.

Not the door you might have left unlocked, not the stranger you might have brushed against, not the bump in the road you might have mistaken for a body.

Now the spotlight swivels inward. The danger isn't external anymore—it's supposedly hiding in your core.

This is the feared possible self: the version of you OCD insists might be lurking just beneath the surface, waiting to be exposed.

Not a random nightmare, not a sudden twist in the plot, but a character meticulously crafted by the same tricks that have been running all along.

The feared self doesn't appear after the bubble forms; it grows out of the very same distortions that built the bubble in the first place.

Every crack in trust, every *what if*, every sandbag of false proof, every echo mistaken for revelation.

All of it lays the groundwork for this moment, when the lie stops feeling like a possibility to check and instead feels like an identity to hide.

And the materials? They're not foreign. OCD raids your own storage.

It takes the values you cherish most, the traits you prize, the lines you've drawn about right and wrong—and bends them until they point back at you like weapons.

- If you don't feel 100% loving right now, maybe you're incapable of love.
- If you can imagine losing control, maybe you're destined to.
- If you had that thought last week, maybe it wasn't just a thought—maybe it revealed who you really are.

It cherry-picks moments from your past, edits them without context, and plays them back with a sinister filter.

It's like finding an old photograph of yourself that's been doctored. The face is yours. The body is yours. But the expression has been altered — and suddenly it tells a story that was never true.

Outside the OCD frame, the fraud is obvious: no proof, no case. Inside the frame, the absence of evidence doesn't acquit you—it condemns you further.

Maybe you're so good at hiding it that there's nothing left to find.

In this courtroom, OCD is both prosecutor and judge, and the rules are stacked against you. Facts are irrelevant. Emotional conviction substitutes for evidence. Urgency replaces reason.

Once the feared self takes hold, everything becomes admissible: thoughts, sensations, flashes of memory.

None of them neutral anymore; all of them potential evidence for the case against you.

The fear isn't just that you *could* cause harm—it's that you are the kind of person who harms. The doubt isn't just about whether your relationship feels right—it's about whether you're even capable of love at all. The discomfort isn't just about contamination—it's about being permanently tainted, irreversibly flawed.

This identity doesn't bloom after the fact. It grows in the same soil as the obsession itself, watered by the same faulty reasoning, fed by the same illusions.

The bubble provides the set; the feared self is the mask you're pressured to wear.

It is the role OCD writes for you without your consent, then pressures you to play as though it's the only script you've ever had.

The faces of this character may vary, but the machinery is always the same:

The Harmful Self: *What if I'm secretly dangerous?*
The Corrupt Self: *What if I'm morally broken?*
The Fraudulent Self: *What if my life is a lie?*
The Defective Self: *What if I'm incapable of connection?*

Each of these masks is sewn from your own material and placed on your face without audition. And once the curtain rises, you're trapped in costume, acting out lines you never chose, convinced the audience is watching for you to slip.

The trick, of course, is that none of it is discovery. It's not a hidden truth being uncovered.

It's just another masterpiece of misdirection—crafted from the same sleight of hand that built the illusion in the first place.

The deeper truth is this: the feared self feels like the climax, but it isn't the whole show. It's the most personal mask in the theatre, but the stage has been built by many hands.

The distrusted senses, the runaway imagination, the sandbags of misapplied reality, the phantom sensations, the canyon of echoes, the suffocating bubble—all of them work together to keep you inside the performance.

In the next chapter, we'll stop watching the performance as willing volunteers and start looking for the wires. We'll trace the seams in every illusion—the cracks in the bubble, the props of phantom evidence, the echoes mistaken for input, the masks of the feared self.

Because the power of a trick isn't in the lie itself, but in our cooperation with it.

Once you glimpse how the act is staged, you also glimpse how to step off the stage.

That's where the spell begins to break.

Key Insights

- OCD doesn't strike in one blow. It stages a performance: distrust, imagination, then misapplied reality.

- Phantom experiences — sensations, thoughts, even "memories' — aren't truths revealed. They're props of absorption.

- The echo chamber effect: outputs get mistaken for inputs. A thought you generate feels like evidence.

- So-called 'intrusive thoughts" aren't random invaders. They're echoes of doubt in motion, artifacts of reasoning drifted from the senses.

- The feared possible self is OCD's most personal illusion — not a hidden identity, but a character woven from your values and fears.

- From the outside, it looks like make-believe. From the inside, it feels like truth. That gap — between illusion and conviction — *is* the entire trick.

The Program: OCD's Stagecraft at a Glance

Before we leave the theatre of illusions, here's the cast list of OCD's tricks laid out side by side. Think of it as a look behind the curtain — a reminder of each act, each sleight of mind, and how it feels from the inside.

Act/Trick	What OCD Does	Metaphor	How It Feels
Distrust of the Senses & Self	Undermines senses, memory, and self-knowledge; pushes you to dig for hidden dangers.	The dam starts to crack.	"What I see or know no longer feels solid."
Boundless Imagination	Let's imagination run untethered — turning abstract possibilities into urgent now-concerns.	The river breaks through.	"Remote maybes feel pressing and relevant."
Misapplied Reality	Stitches facts, values, and previous experiences into the doubt to make it look official.	Sandbags in your living room.	"The doubt feels cemented into reality"
Phantom Experiences	Generates sensations or emotions that mimic the danger.	Special effects on stage.	"I feel it, so it must mean something."
Phantom Thoughts	Scripts phrases, images, or "confessions" that sound self-revealing.	Dialogue scripted by OCD.	"It came up on its own — it must be true."
The Echo Chamber	Produces a thought, then disguises it as fresh input.	Shouting into a canyon.	"The echo feels like a voice in the dark."
The Bubble/ Matrix	Locks you inside a simulation where doubt feels like law.	The blue pill disguised as the red pill.	"The urge to resolve feels inevitable."
The Feared Possible Self	Builds a counterfeit identity from your own material — values, memories, traits.	A doctored photograph; a role you never auditioned for.	"Secret guilt or shame has finally caught up with me."

Try This: Spot the Stagecraft

By now you've seen how obsessional doubts don't land out of nowhere — they're staged. Distrust cracks the dam, imagination floods in, and misapplied fragments of reality stitch the story together until it feels solid. Then come the special effects: sensations, echoes, even counterfeit "selves."

The next time a doubt grips you, pause for a moment. Instead of arguing with the doubt, ask:

- What move is OCD using here?

- Is this distrust of my senses or memory?

- Is this imagination flooding me with "what ifs"?

- Is this reality being misused — a fact or value bent out of shape?

- Or is it one of the special effects — a feeling, image, or echo that only appeared after the doubt began?

- Is this the feared self — a fake character created from my values and fears — being mistaken for my identity?

Don't worry about getting the label perfect. Just noticing *that it's a move at all* is enough. Because once you see it as stagecraft, it starts to lose its authority.

You can use the Program table on the previous page if you'd like a quick reminder of each "act." Think of it as a program note you can return to when the show starts up again.

Chapter 4

Breaking the Illusion

Cracking the Spell: The Sleight of Mind

The magician's central move isn't the one that makes you clap. It's the one you never see — the quiet, perfect misdirection that convinces you something impossible is standing right in front of you.

OCD's master move works the same way. It doesn't make danger likely. It makes it feel *relevant*.

And in the theatre of the mind, relevance always outruns odds.

Think about it:

The chance your child is sick is minuscule. But OCD whispers, *Yes... but they could be,* and suddenly checking becomes an act of love.

The odds you left the stove on are almost zero. But OCD insists, *Yes... but you might have,* and now you're halfway home to make sure.

Normally, imagination stays tethered to reality — a noise at night sparks possible causes, but all linked back to something you actually heard.

OCD cuts that tether. It takes a scene conjured out of thin air and slips it into the same mental space as a real probability.

The trick hides in plain sight — not in mixing imagination and reality, but in letting imagination impersonate reality.

That confusion doesn't begin with panic — it begins with reasoning. The mind performs a subtle sleight of hand long before the body ever feels a thing.

In everyday life, imagination plays a supporting role. You hear a sound and your mind offers possibilities — a falling hanger, a pet moving around, maybe even an intruder — but always anchored to something you sensed.

OCD breaks that natural link. It elevates an abstract *what if* into a pressing *maybe right now.*

Not certainty. Not likelihood. *Relevance.*

That single upgrade turns irrelevance into urgency.

In everyday reasoning, countless "what ifs" never even register — you don't re-test whether gravity still works or re-verify your birthdate, because they stay naturally filtered out.

OCD's move is to hijack that filter — to smuggle one of its fabrications into the "deal-with-this-now" pile — a quiet trick of attention that makes fiction feel urgent.

And the moment that shift happens, ignoring the thought feels reckless — even when the evidence is missing.

That's the sleight of mind. It doesn't enlarge the danger. It enlarges the importance.

It quietly upgrades an imagined possibility into something that feels immediate — and it does it so cleanly, you never see the switch.

You felt the lock click; OCD says, *Treat it as unresolved.* You feel well; OCD says, *Assume there's a hidden illness.*

Nothing about likelihood changed — only the story your mind told about relevance.

And yet... sometimes, you catch a glimmer. It doesn't start with panic. It starts with a pause.

The story has been running in your head for minutes, maybe hours — gathering details, tightening its grip. And then, out of nowhere, there's a flicker. A split-second where something feels... off.

It's like watching a magician for the hundredth time and spotting the faintest glint of a hidden wire. The trick still plays out, but now you know: there's more going on than meets the eye.

Once you spot that wire — the exact moment when the unreal is promoted into the role of the relevant — the spell begins to crack.

Because if the relevance is manufactured, the urgency is an illusion... and the whole structure of the doubt starts to wobble.

That's the real exit. You don't break free by answering OCD's questions. You break free by catching the *promotion* — the instant imagination gets mistaken for importance — and letting the scene collapse before it becomes a story.

Why Relevance Always Wins

People with OCD often ask some version of the same question: *If I know the chances are tiny, why can't I let it go?*

The answer is simple but subtle: because your mind isn't weighing chances. It's weighing relevance.

OCD's sleight of mind doesn't inflate likelihood. It upgrades the irrelevant into the relevant — pulling abstract "maybes" into the mental category of "this is unresolved right now."

Human beings are wired to respond to what feels live in the present moment. If a possibility seems relevant, even the slimmest chance becomes hard to ignore.

That's why a parent can't shrug off the thought, *Maybe I left the baby's window open,* even if they remember closing it. The memory doesn't settle the matter once the doubt is framed as relevant. The only way to resolve it — within the illusion — is to cooperate with it by checking.

The content of the doubt almost doesn't matter. What matters is its apparent status. It feels unresolved, and therefore it feels like it must be acted upon.

Other treatment approaches to OCD notice this too — they tell you not to give importance to the thought.

But here's the deeper truth: the real question isn't *how to treat it as irrelevant*; it's *how it became relevant in the first place.*

Take the typical stove example. Rationally, you know the odds are close to zero. You saw the switch. You remember turning it.

But the moment OCD slips in a whisper — *Yes, but what if you didn't?* — the numbers collapse. Why? Because likelihood is abstract, and abstract doesn't win against the pull of relevance. When something feels like it belongs here and now, probability loses its grip.

It's not that you're convinced the stove is on. It's that you can no longer treat the possibility as irrelevant. It's been reclassified as live — immediate, personal, and demanding.

The same logic applies to the most disturbing kinds of doubts. OCD doesn't just play with stoves and locks. It recruits whatever matters most to you — your morals, your love, your identity — evidence waiting to be examined.

A purely fabricated possibility like *What if I'm secretly dangerous?* isn't experienced as a stray idea. It's reclassified as a case file that demands investigation.

The odds are irrelevant. Once OCD has upgraded it into the category of urgent and unresolved, ignoring it no longer feels safe — it feels reckless, even immoral. That's the cruel magic of relevance: it makes fiction feel like duty.

That's why primary doubts matter more than consequences. Compulsions don't come directly from imagined disasters; they come from the promotion itself.

Without *Maybe I didn't turn the stove off,* the whole house-fire scenario never gets airtime. Without *Maybe I didn't lock the door,* the burglary never enters the imagination.

OCD doesn't need to persuade you that catastrophe is likely. It only needs to persuade you that the first doubt belongs there. Once that happens, everything else follows.

Think of it like an alarm system. If the alarm rings in your house, you respond. You don't pause to calculate the odds of an actual fire. You respond because the sound itself makes the matter feel urgent. The false alarm is indistinguishable from the true alarm at the level of urgency.

OCD exploits this: it rings alarms with no evidence behind them, and your body still reacts as if the signal were valid. The sound feels real enough to justify the motion.

The stove is already off. The door is already locked. Your love is already intact. Your decency and intentions are already intact. But the alarm reframes the matter as unresolved, and your body responds.

From the outside, it looks like overthinking — maybe even a touch of absurdity. Who second-guesses a locked door after hearing the click? Who wonders if gravity still works, or re-checks whether the sun actually rose this morning?

But from the inside, it feels like responsibility. Because once a doubt has been marked as relevant, ignoring it feels reckless. That's the emotional geometry of obsession: relevance outweighs reason.

You can silence the alarm for a moment by checking, reviewing, replaying. But until you see that the alarm itself is false — triggered by imagination, not reality — it will ring again. Reassurance fails not because it's weak, but because it accepts the premise: that the doubt deserved an answer.

Notice, too, how selective this is. You don't obsess about every far-fetched possibility. You don't panic about being struck by lightning each time you step outside, or about the ceiling caving in with every creak. Those possibilities remain abstract.

OCD's cruelty lies in its precision: it chooses specific doubts, ties them to your values and memories, and stamps them with the mark of relevance. Once stamped, they bypass probability and command your attention.

And this is the real cost. The true damage isn't just the wasted hours checking, scrubbing, or replaying. It's the collapse of the ordinary filter that lets you separate what's relevant from what's not. When that filter is broken, reality itself feels negotiable.

The world outside keeps moving in its ordinary rhythm, but inside the bubble, you no longer know what deserves attention and what doesn't.

This is the heart of the illusion. Until it's seen clearly, no amount of probability will ever outweigh the false sense of relevance.

Realization & Implications

When people finally catch the trick, it almost always comes as a surprise. They don't see it while chasing the doubt. They see it when they pause and ask a different kind of question — not *Did I leave the stove on?* but *Why does this doubt feel so urgent when I know I saw the switch?*

That shift is everything.

The moment you recognize that the power of the doubt comes not from evidence but from a false stamp of relevance, the spell begins to loosen. What looked airtight a moment ago starts to loosen, because you can finally see its foundation for what it is — manufactured, not meaningful.

And this has profound implications.

It's not that the doubt is unresolved. It's that the doubt was never entitled to resolution at all.

There is no hidden truth waiting to be uncovered. There's only a sleight of categorization — a fabricated *maybe* slipped into the same box as a real *right now*.

The elaborate tricks described in the last chapter — the erosion of trust, the flood of *what ifs*, the sandbags of misapplied reality, the phantom props and echoing lines — all serve this one end: to elevate imagination to the rank of relevance.

It's not a signal of danger. It's a false elevation — a mirage mistaken for ground. That's the whole illusion.

And here's what realization changes. You stop trying to win the argument. You stop explaining, proving, or checking.

Because you finally see that the doubt was never asking for answers — it was only asking for attention. And once you refuse that invitation, the scene falls apart.

The frame collapses. The story loses its stage.

This realization redefines the whole project. The task is not to settle the doubt, nor to prove it unfounded, nor to tolerate it endlessly. The task is to recognize the category error — a possibility masquerading as a present problem. Once you see that, you no longer owe it an answer.

The shift doesn't always happen in a single flash of clarity. More often, it comes gradually: the same doubt arises again, and each time you notice a little earlier, *Wait, this is the move — this is the point where imagination sneaks in and suddenly feels urgent.*

Every recognition strips another layer from the illusion until, eventually, the whole performance looks thin, flimsy, transparent.

And when that happens, something remarkable follows. Compulsions lose their fuel. You no longer feel driven to re-check the switch, replay the conversation, test your emotions, or scrub your hands, because the doubt that powered those urges no longer carries weight.

It's not that you fought harder. It's that the engine ran out of gas once the false relevance was exposed.

This is the true pivot. OCD is not about uncertainty. It is about mistaking the imagined for the relevant. Once you see that error clearly, the entire logic of obsession collapses.

How This Differs

Every legitimate evidence-based approach to OCD agrees on one thing: obsessions don't deserve the importance they demand.

Exposure and Response Prevention (ERP) asks you to confront your fears, tolerate uncertainty, and resist the pull to ritualize. Acceptance and Commitment Therapy (ACT) teaches you to accept thoughts and feelings without fighting them, noticing them with mindfulness instead of struggle. Appraisal-based CBT focuses on how intrusive thoughts get misread as meaningful and helps you reinterpret those appraisals so the mind stops treating noise as signal.

All of these help. All of them give relief.

But Inference-Based CBT (ICBT) — the treatment approach this book is based on — makes a sharper cut. It doesn't just say, "Treat the thought as irrelevant." It asks: *how did the thought get upgraded into relevance in the first place?*

That promotion isn't random. It doesn't happen just because the thought was shocking or taboo. It happens through a reasoning sequence that starts before the doubt ever appears.

First, OCD plants distrust — *Maybe your memory, your senses, your self-knowledge can't be trusted.* Then imagination steps in, unmoored from reality, and begins drafting scenarios. Finally, scraps of real experience — a feeling, a value, a half-remembered fact — get spliced into the script until the fiction looks official. By the time the doubt arrives, it doesn't feel like a passing idea. It feels like a live case.

That's why ICBT doesn't frame the problem as "uncertainty intolerance." The issue isn't that you can't stand not knowing. The issue is that OCD manufactured a false unknown and smuggled it into the "matters now" pile. What you're wrestling with isn't uncertainty at all — it's misidentification: an imagined "maybe" disguised as a real-time problem.

This is the difference in strategy. ERP asks you to stand in front of the alarm and not run. ACT reminds you the alarm doesn't need fighting — you can watch it without obeying. Appraisal-based CBT shows you the alarm's volume knob is turned up by interpretation. ICBT goes backstage and shows you the wiring — the hidden cue that triggered the scene with no danger behind it.

Once you see that, you don't need to prove yourself safe, and you don't need to endure endless discomfort. You only need to recognize the promotion for what it is: a sleight of mind.

From here, the work shifts. The illusions have been unmasked; what remains is learning how to move through them without stepping back into the script. The five doorways that follow explore that transition — five ways the mind reorients once the show loses its hold.

The Five Doorways Out of OCD

You already know the architecture of the illusion. What comes next is learning to walk through it with your eyes open — not as a believer, but as a witness.

These doorways mark the points where the illusion starts to thin — places where the spell flickers, the wires show, or the scenery loses its depth. They aren't steps or stages. They're shifts in perception — five ways the mind begins to reorient once it stops taking the story at face value.

Each doorway offers a different glimpse of freedom. You don't have to force them open; you only need to notice when you're standing near one. Even a moment of recognition — one clear breath outside the script — is enough to start breaking the continuity of the play.

And once the continuity breaks, so does the urgency. The scene softens. The frame loses its hold. What felt like crisis begins to look like choreography — and you can finally step offstage.

Doorway 1: The Doubt Is 100% Imaginary

Every obsession begins the same way: with a possibility, not with evidence.

"I could have hurt someone without realizing it."
"I might have left the stove on."
"What if I don't really love my partner?"

Notice what's missing: anything anchored to the here and now.

You're not looking at a wounded stranger. You're not standing in front of a burning stove. You're not holding proof that your feelings are gone.

All you have is a thought — a mental simulation. And yet it feels urgent.

This is the first doorway: realizing that obsessional doubts are built entirely from imagination. They don't lean on the senses.

They actively sidestep them. You see the light go out, but the thought says, *Maybe it's still on.* You feel the soap rinse away, but the thought says, *Maybe your hands are still dirty.* OCD dismisses perception to clear space for its imagined storyline.

Think of a courtroom without witnesses, fingerprints, or evidence bags. The entire case rests on a dramatic reenactment played out on screen. That's not evidence. That's theatre.

Catching this doorway doesn't mean dismissing imagination altogether. Imagination is essential in everyday life. It helps us plan, prepare, create. But in OCD, imagination is unmoored from evidence — a compass with no north, spinning wildly until you mistake motion for direction.

The moment you recognize: *This doubt exists only in imagination* — not in perception, not in evidence — the grip loosens. The possibility hasn't vanished, but its stage has been exposed.

Doorway 2: The Doubt Is Entirely Irrelevant

Here's the second move: even if a possibility is imaginable, it does not automatically belong in the present. That distinction — between *could* and *matters now* — is where OCD does its finest editing.

You know the noise upstairs was just footsteps from the neighbor, but OCD insists, *Yes, but what if something got in the house?*

You know your attraction has always been genuine, but OCD whispers, *Yes, but what if it isn't anymore?*

It's not arguing for likelihood. It's arguing for relevance. And once something feels relevant, ignoring it feels reckless.

You can tell yourself the chances are small, but until you recognize the irrelevance, the doubt remains sticky. Because the moment OCD says, *Yes, but what if this time?* the odds become irrelevant too.

Think of an actor forgetting their line in a play. The slip is tiny, but the spotlight lingers on it, and suddenly the moment feels central, weighty, demanding resolution. The play itself hasn't changed — only your sense of relevance has.

This is why OCD doesn't target every far-fetched scenario. This is why OCD doesn't fixate on every remote danger. You don't panic that a loose leaf on the street signals a storm, or that a flicker in a lightbulb means the house will burn down. Those possibilities stay distant, uninvited. But OCD chooses specific doubts — ones tied to your values, memories, or moral sense — and stamps them with false relevance.

Spotting this doorway means pausing to ask: *Does this doubt actually belong in this moment? Or has OCD simply pulled it into relevance by sleight of hand?*

When you see that irrelevance clearly, the urgency fades. The doubt may still whisper, but it no longer commands the stage.

Doorway 3: The Doubt Is Fundamentally False

Every obsession runs on staged reasoning — a small sequence of tricks that makes imagination look like investigation. The logic isn't random; it's rehearsed, and it always follows the same rhythm.

It begins with undermining perception — *Even if I saw it clearly, maybe I missed something.*

That tiny fracture opens the stage for imagination to take the lead — *If I can picture it, maybe it happened.*

Then comes the misuse of reality's props — selective facts, memories, or values borrowed from everyday life and stitched into the scene as evidence.

Once the story feels assembled, later tricks start to keep it alive: phantom sensations, echoes, and finally the reversal of cause and effect, where the doubt's own by-products are mistaken for proof that the danger was real all along.

Each move feeds the next. What began as an abstract, irrelevant possibility becomes a scenario, then a suspicion, then a verdict. By the time the full set is running, it no longer feels like reasoning at all — it feels like discovery.

This doorway isn't about debating the content of a thought; it's about seeing the machinery that made it feel convincing.

Whenever you catch imagination promoted to evidence, fragments of reality turned into confirmation, or an echo mistaken for a clue, you're watching the staged logic unfold.

It's like catching a math error in the first line of a long equation — you don't need to check every step that follows. Once you see how the case was built, you stop believing the verdict. The illusion loses its footing the moment the first false move is exposed.

This recognition doesn't answer the doubt. It dissolves its legitimacy.

Doorway 4: OCD Is Not About Uncertainty

For decades, OCD has been framed as a problem of "intolerance of uncertainty." The advice is often: *learn to live with doubt or not being certain.*

There's a surface truth there — OCD does feel uncertain. But that's the illusion. From an ICBT perspective, OCD isn't driven by uncertainty; it's driven by misidentification.

The doubts you're trying to "tolerate" aren't genuine unknowns. They're *false problems* — imagined scenarios made to feel relevant.

This is like asking someone to "tolerate uncertainty" about whether the earth is flat. You could train yourself to shrug at the question, but the real shift comes when you realize the premise was invalid to begin with.

That's why this doorway matters. The issue isn't learning to stomach endless unknowns. The issue is recognizing when the unknown itself is fake.

You don't need to practice "living with the doubt" that maybe you touched your baby inappropriately while changing a diaper. You need to recognize that this doubt was never a question to begin with — it's an imagined accusation, irrelevant and without basis. Once you see that, there's nothing left to tolerate.

Yes, OCD always comes with a feeling of uncertainty — but that's part of the trick. The doubt manufactures that feeling first, then points to it as proof that something must be resolved. The sensation of *I can't be sure* isn't a sign of low tolerance for uncertainty — it's the by-product of a false alarm.

Doorway 5: There Is Nothing to Resolve

The final doorway brings the whole picture into focus.

If the doubt is imaginary...
If it is irrelevant...

If it is built on false reasoning...
If it was never about real uncertainty...

Then what remains? Nothing.

And that's the point.

There was never a real problem to solve. Every compulsion —
every check, every confession, every review, every mental
rehearsal — is built on the premise that there is a solvable issue
at hand. But once you see the structure, you recognize the truth:
the "problem" never existed outside the illusion.

This doorway doesn't mean you've answered the doubt. It means
you've withdrawn the only thing keeping it alive: cooperation.

Think of it like a magician waiting for applause after the trick. The
only reason the illusion continues is because the audience plays
along. The moment you stop clapping, the performance ends.

That's what stepping through the fifth doorway feels like. Not a
dramatic battle. Not a triumph over the doubt. Simply the
realization: *there is nothing here to resolve.*

And with that, the stage goes dark.

Key Insights

- OCD's master trick is not making dangers likely — it's
  making them relevant. Once a possibility feels like it
  belongs in the here and now, the odds no longer matter.

- That shift comes from confusion: imagination slipping into
  the same mental category as perception. Abstract "what ifs"
  masquerade as present probabilities.

- Relevance always outruns reason. A faint possibility that
  feels urgent will command more attention than a real
  danger that feels abstract.

- Realization is the pivot. Once you see the doubt's power comes from manufactured relevance, the urgency begins to collapse. The stage props lose their authority.

- The five doorways (imaginary, irrelevant, false, not about uncertainty, nothing to resolve) are vantage points — each one shows you the wires of the trick and gives you a way to step out of the theatre.

Try This: Walk Through the Doorways

OCD's trick isn't that it makes danger likely — it makes it feel relevant *now.* The five doorways in this chapter are ways to catch that promotion in action.

Next time a doubt arises, pause for a moment and simply ask yourself:

- Does this doubt have any anchor in present reality, or is it built from imagination alone?

- Does this thought actually belong in this moment — or is OCD just stamping it with false relevance?

- What reasoning trick is being used here — leading you to confuse imagination with reality, or phantom sensations as evidence?

- Is this a real unknown to live with, or a fake problem built from nothing?

- If all of that is true...does it really need resolving at all?

You don't have to write it down or walk through every doorway each time. Even catching one is enough to loosen the grip.

The point isn't to settle the doubt — it's to see how it was staged. And when you glimpse that, the performance starts to collapse.

Chapter 5

Everyday Freedom

The Air Outside

When you've been inside an illusion long enough, freedom doesn't arrive with fanfare. It arrives with space.

Think of walking out of a crowded theatre after a long, gripping performance. For hours, you've been in the dark—every sound, every light, every movement designed to hold your attention. The story is so immersive you forget the seats, the stage, even yourself.

Then the doors open.

Cool air hits your face. The street sounds are ordinary, almost boring compared to the spectacle inside. But that ordinariness is what feels like release.

You're no longer tracking every line, every cue. The world is happening without you needing to solve it.

That's what everyday freedom from OCD feels like. Not a thunderclap of insight, not a once-and-for-all victory, but the quiet relief of stepping outside the theatre and realizing the show was never mandatory in the first place.

Inside the bubble, everything feels charged. Thoughts arrive like breaking news, each one demanding analysis. A staging note masquerades as evidence; a flicker of doubt feels like a court summons. You're absorbed, scanning for meaning, bracing for impact.

Step outside the bubble, and the same world looks utterly different. A locked door is just a locked door, not a question. A moment of impatience is just that — impatience, not a sign of failing character.

The air feels flatter, quieter, even boring—but it's the kind of boring that lets you breathe.

In Chapter 4 you caught the wires—the promotion trick that turns a made-up "maybe" into a "matters now." If that was spotting the glitch in the Matrix, this chapter is the unplug.

No boss fight, no dramatic monologue—just daylight returning, shoulders dropping, the hum of unstaged life.

This chapter is about what happens next: living in that space on purpose.

Because clarity isn't only noticing the trick; it's practicing not sitting back down once you've stood.

We'll name the bubble for what it is, then practice the simple art that keeps you outside: reality sensing—trusting the click, the sight, the hand you're holding—without handing the microphone back to imagination.

The bubble still exists. The Matrix still hums in the background. The theatre still advertises its next show.

The difference is practical: you don't buy the ticket. You don't walk through the doors.

And once you know what it feels like to stay outside, the ordinariness of reality begins to feel extraordinary—a relief so steady it barely needs words.

Reality never left. It was always there, humming underneath the performance. Stepping out isn't conjuring a new world — it's remembering the one that was already waiting.

Two Worlds Running at Once

When you're inside OCD's bubble, it doesn't feel like you're in an illusion. It feels like you're in the only world that counts.

Every thought buzzes with importance, every doubt feels like a live broadcast. The atmosphere is taut, insistent — like you've been tuned into a private channel that never goes off-air.

But here's the strange thing: that world isn't the only one running. Right alongside it, ordinary life is still happening. The kettle boils, the cat stretches, the street outside moves in its steady rhythm. Reality hasn't gone anywhere — it's just been covered by the set.

Think of it like The Matrix. The simulation doesn't create a new planet; it overlays one. The machinery projects a world full of drama and danger, while the real world continues humming quietly underneath. OCD works the same way. The bubble doesn't erase reality — it superimposes a charged, fabricated version of it.

Inside the bubble, a door click becomes a riddle, a fleeting image a prophecy, a forgotten detail, a moral indictment. Outside the bubble, the same events look plain, even dull: the door locked, the image passed, the detail was just a detail.

That dullness is the giveaway. Reality is usually quiet, steady, sometimes even boring. The bubble is noisy, inflated, insistent.

One is theatre. The other is documentary.

One is CGI — computer-generated imagery, the digital special effects used to make illusions look real. The other is daylight.

And here's the pivot: the two realities don't alternate like light switches. They run *together*.

At any given moment, you can notice the hum of the bubble or the ordinariness outside. The exit isn't about creating freedom out of thin air. It's about remembering which world is real — and stepping toward it, even if just for a moment.

Everyday Freedom in Practice

Everyday freedom doesn't look heroic. It doesn't make headlines or earn applause. In fact, it often passes unnoticed — which is precisely what makes it so different from the theatre inside the bubble.

Inside the bubble, life becomes performance. Every gesture feels monitored, every moment evaluated for hidden meaning.

Outside the bubble, the script dissolves. The same moments are still there — but they no longer carry the spotlight.

It's turning off the tap, hearing the last drop fall, and trusting the stillness that follows. No inspection, no second-guessing the sound. Just turning, drying, walking away.

It's hugging your child without scanning your feelings for proof of love, without turning tenderness into a test. The hug is simply a hug — soft fabric, warm body, breath against your chest.

It's finishing an email, hearing the little *whoosh* as it sends, and moving on to the next task without circling back to reread every line.

It's reading a headline without spinning it into a prophecy about your future.

In short, it's ordinary life — ordinary because it isn't distorted, and extraordinary because of the relief that comes with that ordinariness.

Freedom doesn't add fireworks. It subtracts the noise. What's left is often quiet, plain, even dull compared to the adrenaline of OCD. But that ordinariness is exactly the point. It's solid. It holds.

Think of it like gravity. You don't notice it most of the time, but it keeps you steady. Everyday freedom is the same — not a thrill but a rhythm. The kind that lets you show up for your life without having to check whether you're doing it right.

The world doesn't feel brighter; it feels *truer*. And that truth — ordinary, steady, lived — is what healing actually sounds like.

Reality Sensing

If the bubble is the theatre, then reality sensing is stepping out into daylight and letting your eyes adjust. It's not mystical, it's not meditation, and it doesn't require hours of training.

It's simply learning to rely on what is directly in front of you, instead of being pulled into what your imagination insists might be happening.

OCD thrives on a gap — the small crack between what your senses already confirm and the endless stories your imagination can spin around it. Reality sensing is about closing that gap, letting perception carry more weight than performance.

Take the front door. You turn the key, hear the bolt slide, feel the resistance, maybe even see the lock in place. That's four solid pieces of reality: sight, sound, touch, movement.

Yet in the bubble, one whisper of *But what if it didn't really lock?* suddenly outweighs them all. You're not doubting the lock. You're doubting your senses. Reality sensing is about letting the testimony stand.

Or driving. Your hands grip the wheel, the road hums beneath the tires, the speedometer needle hovers steadily. That's reality. But in the bubble, you replay the thought: *What if I hit someone and didn't notice?*

Notice how this doubt requires you to abandon every piece of direct evidence. Reality sensing is choosing the world you're actually in, not the one imagination is scripting in parallel.

Cooking works the same way. You turn off the burner and hear the click. You see the red glow fade. You feel the cool metal of the knob under your fingers. That's three confirmations. Yet the bubble insists: *But what if it's still on? What if you didn't really turn it all the way?* The whisper is theatre. The confirmations are reality.

Relationships, too. You hold your partner's hand. That's reality: skin, warmth, presence. But the bubble whispers: *What if you don't really love them? What if this feeling isn't real?*

Reality sensing doesn't argue. It returns to the facts already present — the hand in yours, the conversation you shared, the life you're building. Love isn't a courtroom verdict. It's lived reality, moment by moment.

Even a headline can pull you back into the theatre: *Scientists warn of possible new virus strain.* Inside the bubble, this becomes catastrophe: *What if I'm already infected? What if I'll cause disaster?*

Reality sensing brings you home — to the couch, the light from the window, the steady rhythm of your breath. You can act on facts when they matter — wash your hands, see a doctor if you're sick — but you don't have to follow imagination into prophecy.

Work, hygiene, daily routines — the principle holds. The clean smell of soap. The cool laptop lid shutting. These are all anchors. The bubble always whispers its *what ifs*. Reality sensing lets what's in front of you carry more weight.

And it doesn't stop with outer senses. Inner senses — hunger that says it's time to eat, fatigue that says it's time to rest, the warmth in your chest when you laugh, the calm after finishing a task — are also testimony. In the bubble, they're constantly mistranslated: *If I feel tense, maybe the danger is real. If I don't feel overwhelming love every second, maybe it isn't real.*

Reality sensing lets those inner cues be what they are. Tiredness is tiredness. Tension is tension. Calm is calm. They don't need courtroom interpretation.

Try it playfully. A cup of coffee is enough. Feel the weight in your hand, the warmth against your skin, the aroma rising. That's reality. A thought like *What if it's poisoned?* can always intrude, but reality sensing answers: *this is the cup, this is the warmth, this is the smell.* This is the world you're in.

Imagination isn't the enemy. It's the special effects department — the CGI in your mind. The danger isn't that it exists; the danger is when you forget it's CGI and start treating it as the real film you're living in.

Reality sensing doesn't banish imagination, nor does it abandon thought. It simply puts them back in their rightful role — tools for creativity, not substitutes for evidence.

Start small. Let the click of the stove knob be enough. Let the sound of the lock be the end of the matter. Let the warmth of a hug or the weight of a coffee cup carry its own meaning, without handing the microphone back to imagination.

It won't feel dramatic. It may even feel simple — almost too simple — compared to OCD's theatre.

But simplicity is the strength here. Each time you trust what's real, the stage lights dim a little more, and the world comes back into focus — solid, quiet, and unmistakably yours.

Ladder of Ease

Reality sensing aims you back toward ease. The "work" isn't to push harder; it's to stop adding effort—no extra checks, no mental replays, no second passes.

Think of this as a ladder you climb by doing less, not more. Each rung is a small permission to let what's already clear be enough.

The work is also not to confront fears. The fears are not real to start with—they're projections of imagination mistaken for reality. What you're reclaiming isn't courage against danger, but *trust in what's actually here.*

On the lowest rungs are the easy anchors. Turning off the light and watching the bulb fade. Pouring a glass of water and feeling the weight shift in your hand. These are small, everyday actions where your senses give instant, unambiguous feedback. No courtroom required.

A step higher are the ordinary but slightly stickier moments. Locking the front door once and walking away without circling back. Turning off the stove, hearing the click, and letting the click stand as final. These are the places where OCD usually slips in a whisper — *But what if this time...* — but where your senses still speak clearly if you give them the microphone.

Higher still are the rungs that involve absence — moments where there's nothing left to see, hear, or touch, and imagination rushes to fill the gap. Driving away without replaying every bump in the road. Sending an email without rereading it twenty times. Hugging your child without scanning your feelings for hidden verdicts.

These rungs feel harder because they lack a clear sensory cue — no switch click, no lock turning, no visual proof. In these moments, your senses have already spoken—you're simply practicing trusting their last word, even when there's nothing new to sense. The quiet that follows isn't uncertainty; it's simply the sound of reality no longer needing to speak. The absence of catastrophe is its own testimony.

The top rungs aren't about acrobatics. They're about consistency. You don't leap to the top in one bound. You climb in small movements, one rung at a time, repeating them until your footing feels natural.

Each time you choose to stop at *click, sight, touch — done*, you strengthen your trust in reality. Each time you walk away without replaying, you loosen the bubble's grip.

This ladder isn't about gritting your teeth or "tolerating doubt." It's about *trust economy*: spending less attention on imagination and leaving more with reality.

Navigating the Bubble: Common Slips & Re-Anchors

Even outside the bubble, the pull is strong. You can still find yourself drifting toward the show without realizing you've bought a ticket. The slips are subtle.

You linger too long at the door, staring at the lock as if sight could silence imagination. You jiggle the knob, not to test it but to quiet the whisper that says you didn't. That's not sensing reality anymore. That's feeding the prosecutor new exhibits.

Or you treat a thought like curiosity. *What if this isn't just OCD? What if this time it matters?* It feels like a reasonable question. It isn't. It's the trapdoor back into the theatre, disguised as philosophy.

Or you catch a phantom sensation — a flicker in your chest, a blur in memory — and lean in as if squinting harder will make it settle. But the harder you stare, the slipperier it gets. Phantom evidence thrives on attention.

Sometimes the slip is a line in your head, dark and sudden: *I wanted that. Maybe I meant it.* It feels heavier than an ordinary thought because it arrives dressed as revelation. But it's the same trick — imagination with a mask on.

The re-anchor isn't about resisting or tolerating the thought. It's about remembering what you already know: the doubt is false, born entirely of imagination, irrelevant to the present.

From that knowing, you simply return to where you actually are — sitting on the couch, hand on the mug, life moving forward.

Anchors are simple. They don't argue. They just hold.

The bolt slides, you hear the click, you feel the key resist. *Done.*

The email whooshes, the draft disappears. *Done.*

A hand in yours, skin and warmth. *Done.*

The cup warms your palm, steam rises, the smell is sharp. *Done.*

You don't need to fight the whispers. You don't need to stare them down. Just return to the anchor, name it, and move on.

The bubble survives on loitering. The longer you linger in its doorway — checking, wondering, replaying — the more convincing the show feels

The fastest exit is also the simplest: no loitering.

Saboteur Thoughts

Even when you anchor, OCD doesn't quit. It sends in saboteurs. Not loud alarms, but quiet lines that sound reasonable:

- *What if ignoring this is reckless?*
- *What if real responsibility means checking one more time?*
- *What if freedom is just denial?*
- *What if the very fact you want to stop proves you're hiding something?*

These aren't questions. They're hooks. They don't seek answers. They seek to pull you back into the play.

The trick is familiar by now. OCD takes your best values — honesty, responsibility, love — and forges counterfeits. It stamps them with the seal of conscience. Suddenly the doubt is no longer about a stove or a door. It's about your character. About whether you're reckless, dishonest, unloving.

Sometimes the sabotage goes deeper:

If you were truly good, you wouldn't even need to anchor.
If you were honest, you wouldn't want to look away.
If you really loved, you would feel certain already.

These are feared-self saboteurs — the kind that don't just question your actions, but question *you*.

But that "voice of conscience" is theatre. A doctored line. A phantom confession dressed up as testimony. It feels weighty because OCD echoes it in the cathedral of your mind, where everything sounds louder. But weight is not truth. It's architecture.

The move is simple: name the trick. Say it plain — this is sabotage. That's all. Once you see it as part of the act, it loses its authority.

Then return to the anchor, and walk forward. No courtroom, no verdict — just the next step.

The Rhythm of Stepping Out

Freedom doesn't follow one script. For some, it arrives in a flash — a single moment of clarity that pops the bubble for good. For others, it's slower, steadier — a rhythm learned over time. Either way, it's rarely a single, cinematic ending where you never hear from OCD again.

The bubble will keep advertising its shows. Some days you'll glance at the poster. Some days you'll even wander back inside. That's not failure — it's part of the rhythm.

Think of it like learning the exits in a maze. At first, you spend hours lost in the corridors, convinced there's no way out. Then one day, you stumble across a door. The next time, you still get lost — but you find the door faster. Eventually, you stop panicking when you're inside, because you know there's always a way out.

Or picture a wave. At the beginning, every swell knocks you off your feet. You thrash, tumble, come up gasping. But with practice, you learn to spot the break, to let the water carry you, to stand again. The waves don't stop coming. You just stop drowning in them.

And sometimes the rhythm shifts again: you don't even get pulled under. You see the swell forming, you feel the tug of the riptide, and instead of fighting it later, you step aside before it drags you in.

This is another kind of freedom — not just escaping the bubble, but declining the ticket in the first place.

This is the rhythm of stepping out. You notice when the bubble pulls you in — the sudden urgency, the courtroom cross-exams, the sense that a verdict must be reached. Instead of treating that urgency as truth, you remind yourself: *Ah, I'm in the bubble again.*

That recognition itself is already one foot out the door. And over time, sometimes you'll catch the trick even earlier: *Ah, the bubble is calling me in — but I don't need to enter.*

Sometimes you'll walk right back into daylight. Other times you'll linger, listening to the show a little longer. Both count as progress.

The skill isn't staying out forever. The skill is noticing sooner, stepping out quicker, and, when you can, not stepping in at all.

That rhythm — in, notice, out, decline — is freedom. Not perfect, not permanent for everyone, but for some, it is — the bubble pops, the spell breaks, and it never quite rebuilds. For others, it unfolds gradually — each step a little clearer, each return a little faster.

You stop measuring success by how often the bubble appears, and start measuring by how easily you step outside — and how often you simply keep walking past the door.

Pause here for a moment. Where in your own life have you already stumbled on an exit?

Maybe you caught yourself mid-check and chose not to repeat it. Maybe you noticed the courtroom tone of OCD and thought, *Wait — this feels familiar.*

Those little recognitions are exits. And the more you spot them, the more the maze feels navigable, the more the tide feels crossable, the more the bubble feels optional.

Whether it bursts in an instant or fades through practice, freedom always begins the same way: with seeing the illusion for what it is.

Key Insights

- Everyday freedom isn't dramatic. It's the quiet ordinariness of life without a stage, without a script, without a courtroom.
- The bubble doesn't erase reality. It overlays it. Ordinary life is always running alongside the theatre — the kettle boiling, the door clicking, the hand you're holding.
- Reality sensing means trusting what's directly in front of you — sight, sound, touch, even inner senses like hunger or calm — rather than handing the microphone back to imagination's CGI.
- Anchors are simple: *click—done, whoosh—done, hand in hand—done.* No debate, no courtroom appeal.

- Progress follows a ladder of ease: start small with clear sensory anchors, then climb toward harder triggers. It's not about tolerating doubt, but trusting clarity.

- Slips happen: staring too long, replaying, chasing phantom sensations. The correction is simple — re-anchor, name the trick, move on. No loitering in the doorway.

- Saboteur thoughts disguise themselves as conscience — *What if ignoring this is reckless?* — but they are counterfeits. Naming them strips their weight.

- Freedom can strike in a moment or build through practice. For some, the bubble pops and stays gone; for others, it softens and fades with each step out. Either way, ordinary life becomes home ground again.

Try This: Sensing the Ordinary

Everyday freedom doesn't arrive with fireworks. It shows up in small, steady moments that don't demand anything from you.

The next time OCD leans in with a *what if, maybe, could be, might be*, or *perhaps*, pause and notice what's already here. The click of the lock. The whoosh of the email. The warmth of a hand in yours. The smell of your coffee. That's reality — simple, unadorned, already complete.

At first, the ordinary may feel flat, even boring compared to OCD's theatre. But that very plainness is the signal you've stepped outside the bubble. Theatre is noisy. Reality is quiet. Theatre inflates. Reality holds.

Start small. Let the click of the switch, the snap of the laptop, or the warmth of a cup be enough. The more you let the ordinary stand on its own, the more everyday life feels like fresh air — steady, breathable, real.

Chapter 6

Seeing Through the Feared Possible Self

The Mask You Never Auditioned For

Imagine walking into a theater only to find your name on the program. The curtains rise, the lights hit your face, and suddenly you're on stage in a role you never auditioned for.

Worse, it's not a flattering role — it's the villain, the fraud, the danger everyone whispers about. The lines don't fit, the costume chafes, but the audience stares as if it must be true: this is who you really are.

That's what the feared possible self feels like. OCD doesn't just cast doubts about appliances, germs, or doors. At some point, it turns the spotlight inward and says:

The real danger isn't out there. It's you.

It's the moment OCD stages a scene of blurting something cruel to a child, complete with shock, guilt, and imagined fallout. The script doesn't pause to ask questions — it leaps straight to the role:

Villain. You're handed the mask of someone dangerous, even though your real life shows the opposite.

Then there's the time you forgot to reply to an email, and OCD mutters: *Fraud.* The missed message is woven into a story of incompetence and deception, until you're in costume as the imposter, waiting to be exposed.

Sometimes it's quieter. You notice you don't feel a surge of affection in a particular moment, and OCD whispers: *Loveless.* A single flat note gets exaggerated into a whole score, and suddenly you're playing the role of someone incapable of love — never mind the hundreds of hugs, conversations, and acts of care that make up your real life.

And sometimes it's darker. OCD sketches a disturbing possibility, then splices together fragments from past lapses and imagined scenarios, hissing: *Corrupt.* The mask insists you're morally broken, even though the very reason the scene unsettles you is because you value integrity so deeply.

None of these roles are chosen. None are earned. They're slapped on, mid-performance, by OCD's stage manager. You don't recall rehearsing them, but once the mask is on, it feels glued to your skin.

And here is the trick: the feared self doesn't come across like a fleeting worry. It doesn't feel like, *Maybe I'm coming down with a cold.* It feels like a verdict. A revelation. As if OCD had finally pulled back the curtain to show you who you really are.

That's why the feared self is so sticky. You're not just doubting an action or an object — you're doubting your core. And once that spotlight hits, you start scanning the script, desperate to prove you don't belong in the role. You rehearse counterarguments. You beg for reassurance. You try to peel off the mask. But the more you fight it, the more convincing the show feels.

The truth? It was never your show to begin with.

The feared self is not your character. It is not an unveiling of something hidden. It's a costume, pulled from OCD's wardrobe and forced onto you mid-scene.

A prop, not a portrait. A mask, not a mirror.

The Costume Department

Every illusionist needs a wardrobe. OCD has one too — a costume department stocked with masks and roles, ready to throw onto you at a moment's notice.

The feared self is not a discovery of who you are. It's a production.

The same machinery that inflates an irrelevant and abstract possibility into urgency also stitches those fragments into character masks. Distrust of the senses, untethered imagination, fragments of memory, and manufactured relevance — all feed the wardrobe. By the time you notice, you're already on stage, blinking into the spotlight, wondering how you got there.

The trick works because the costumes are convincing. They are pieced together from real scraps — a lapse here, a hesitation there, a fragment of memory — but they are dyed darker, reshaped, and staged until they look like a verdict. OCD doesn't invent material out of nowhere. It raids your closet.

That flash of irritation with your child gets woven into the costume of the *Dangerous Parent*. Forgetting a work detail is hemmed into the *Irresponsible Fraud*. Not feeling a rush of affection in a hug becomes the mask of the *Loveless Partner*. A stray word that came out wrong is refitted into the *Deceitful Friend*.

And then come the subtler costumes. A passing hollowness is stretched into the mask of the *Empty Self*. A slow day becomes the *Boring Self*. An awkward laugh becomes the *Theatrical Self* who fakes every gesture. A burst of energy is recast as the *Intense Self* who overwhelms everyone. A missed cue in conversation becomes the *Inept Self* who can't manage life.

In ordinary daylight, these fitted masks lose their sheen. Unstaged life doesn't sustain them.

The costumes vary, but the method is the same: OCD picks what you value most, or where you already feel tender or uncertain — new parenthood, new responsibilities, new relationships — and stitches those insecurities into the role you'd least want to play. Then it glues the mask to your face and insists: *This was always you. We're not dressing you up — we're showing the truth.*

That's why feared selves feel so intimate and devastating. They don't strike at random. They are tailored, designed to hit where you care most, or where you feel least sure of yourself. They're cut from your values, fitted to your identity, staged to feel like revelation.

But costumes, no matter how snug they feel, are always temporary. They come from outside, not inside. They can be removed, hung back on the rack, exposed for what they are: stage props.

The feared self is one of OCD's most persuasive tricks because it hides the costume department. It makes you believe the mask was welded to your skin when it was only ever strapped on.

And the exit begins the moment you see the trick for what it is —
not a revelation of hidden identity, but a wardrobe dressed up as
truth.

How Values Become Weapons

Every play needs raw material. The feared self doesn't emerge out
of nothing. It is stitched from the very things you hold most dear.

OCD doesn't accuse you with alien material — it works with your
own values, the ones you prize most. Love, honesty, morality,
responsibility. Instead of applauding them, it drags them into the
costume department and tailors them into weapons.

- Because you value honesty, it sneers: *If you were truly
  honest, you'd confess every doubt. The fact you hesitate
  proves you're deceitful.*

- Because you value morality, it charges: *If you were truly
  good, you wouldn't even imagine that scenario. The fact
  you did means you are corrupt.*

- Because you value responsibility, it scolds: *If you were
  responsible, you'd keep checking, just to be absolutely
  sure. The fact you stopped proves you're reckless.*

The accusations sting because they arrive dressed in the language
of your conscience. They sound like moral verdicts, not imaginary
lines. The feared self is persuasive precisely because it
weaponizes what matters most.

Take love. A parent holds their child, maybe tired, maybe
distracted, and doesn't feel the rush of warmth they expect. OCD
seizes the moment: *Why don't you feel it? What if this means
something darker?*

Reasoning supplies the twist — *if warmth can be absent, maybe its opposite lurks beneath*. Imagination enters next, sketching scenes of harm, and suddenly the parent is accused of being dangerous at their core. What began as ordinary fatigue is rewritten as a mask of menace.

Then another domain: honesty. You've built your life on truth, but one uncertain memory catches. OCD circles it: *If you can't recall clearly, maybe you're hiding something*. From there, hesitation becomes suspect, and imagination supplies the lines of confession. A passing gap of memory is turned into the mask of the *Deceiver*.

Or morality. You recoil from cruelty because it breaks everything you stand for. OCD twists the recoil: *Why recoil so sharply unless cruelty is part of you?* The very proof of conscience is converted into suspicion. Now you're accused of corruption itself.

Or responsibility. You forget a small detail, or you walk away after locking the door. OCD pounces: *If you missed that, maybe you're careless by nature. If you don't check again, maybe disaster proves you reckless.* What was ordinary diligence is rewritten as negligence.

But values aren't the only raw material. OCD also exploits insecurities — the places where you already feel shaky.

A new parent, already unsure if they're doing it right, finds every flash of fatigue or frustration folded into the costume of the *Neglectful Parent*. A student on their first job is handed the mask of the *Incompetent Fraud* after forgetting one small detail. A partner who feels unsteady in intimacy finds every flat moment recast as the *Loveless Self.*

This is why the feared self feels targeted rather than random. OCD doesn't scatter its accusations everywhere — it zeroes in on where you care most, and where you already doubt yourself. The illusionist performs under your brightest spotlight.

This is the genius — and the cruelty — of the feared self. It doesn't pull costumes from a stranger's closet. It rummages through your own wardrobe and turns your best garments inside out.

The result is a mask stitched from your deepest values, now inverted into evidence against you.

That's why the feared self feels so intimate, so devastating. It strikes at the heart of who you most hope to be — and who you most fear you might not be.

It doesn't just question your actions; it questions the very compass you rely on to guide them. It says: *Not only might you fail — you are failure. Not only might you sin — you are corruption itself. Not only might you make a mistake — you are a fraud at your core.*

And once that verdict is whispered, it doesn't feel like imagination. It feels like conscience. It feels like revelation.

Why It Feels Like Revelation

The feared self is persuasive not only because it borrows your values, but because it parades its verdicts as revelation.

It doesn't just hand you a mask and say, *Try this role.* It insists: *This was always your role. We've finally unmasked you.*

This is why the feared self feels different from everyday doubts. Doubting whether you turned off the stove feels like a question. Doubting whether you are a fraud feels like a disclosure — as if the curtain has lifted and you've been exposed.

But what looks like revelation is really fabrication. OCD manufactures "evidence" the way a theatre produces stage props: convincing, weighty, designed to fool the senses — but false all the same.

Heaviness is not truth. The weight you feel in feared-self thoughts comes not from revelation but from construction — the scaffolding of OCD's inner stage, built to echo back your own fears until they sound like prophecy.

And this is why reassurance always fails: it doesn't settle the case but confirms the trial, ratifying the false premise that something about your identity is owed to judgment.

Here's how that manufactured "revelation" takes shape: first, ordinary memories get re-edited into incriminating scenes; second, imagination supplies phantom confessions; third, the echo of moral seriousness is mistaken for conscience.

Doctored Memories

A neutral memory is replayed until it feels incriminating. You recall tucking your child into bed, and suddenly a flicker of doubt inserts itself: *Did I touch them wrong? Did I hesitate too long?*

The scene is replayed in your mind's eye, edited frame by frame, until you're no longer watching the memory but a doctored version, forged in OCD's cutting room.

The trick works because memory itself is fragile. We know memories shift with each recall. OCD exploits that pliability. It overlays doubt, splices in hesitation, adds shadows where none existed.

What was once a warm moment is re-presented as a crime scene. And the more you replay it, the more convincing the doctored version feels, until the real memory is crowded out entirely.

Phantom Confessions

Then there are the phantom confessions — lines that arrive as if they were buried admissions. A sudden voice in your head mutters: *I wanted that. I enjoyed that. I planned that.*

Not because you did, but because imagination can fabricate dialogue as easily as a playwright scripts lines for a character.

These lines land hardest when they strike your insecurities. A parent terrified of being careless hears: *You wanted to harm.* A partner uneasy about intimacy hears: *You never really loved.* A conscientious worker hears: *You wanted to fail.*

The content shifts, but the staging is the same: a counterfeit line dropped into your script, dressed as an admission.

And once the line is written, it feels like it must have come from somewhere. But where? You search your past, you probe your motives, and in that searching, OCD has already won. You're treating a phantom as if it were sworn testimony.

Echoes Mistaken for Conscience

OCD also recruits the echo chamber of conscience itself. A thought feels heavy, serious, morally charged — and you mistake the weight for truth.

After all, ordinary imagination is light, playful, whimsical. But this feels different. This feels grave.

It's like hearing a voice in a cathedral. The acoustics make it echo, resonate, expand — but the echo is not proof of divine authority. It's proof of architecture.

The solemnity of a feared-self thought is not a window into your identity. It's an acoustic trick — the same line, amplified by the vaults of OCD's theatre.

And the more insecure or self-critical you already feel, the more thunderous the echo becomes.

The False Prophet Effect

The net result is what could be called the false prophet effect.

OCD doesn't speak in whispers of possibility. It speaks in the tones of prophecy: *This is who you are. We've seen behind the mask. The truth is revealed.*

And because it speaks with such conviction, you forget to ask: *Where is the evidence? Where is the reality check?*

Instead, you treat imagination's special effects as though they were sworn testimony.

The feared self is persuasive because it forges documents and then stamps them with the seal of conscience. It edits memories into confessions. It scripts phantom admissions. It uses echo and urgency to mimic authority.

But like any forgery, the cracks show when you look closely. The signatures don't match.

The ink is still wet. The "truth" is not a revelation at all — it is a counterfeit. Heavy enough to frighten, slick enough to convince, but still hollow when handled.

The costume looks welded on under the spotlight. In daylight, it falls apart in your hands.

The Feared Self Network

On the surface, OCD looks like it has many faces. One day it's about germs. Another day it's about doors. Later it's about a doubt in your relationship, or a flicker in your memory.

It can feel like the doubts keep multiplying, each one a brand-new obsession.

But underneath the variety lies a single hub. The themes are just spokes on the wheel, all pointing back to the same feared self. The content rotates — the identity accusation repeats.

Take contamination. You wash your hands after touching a doorknob. OCD mutters: *What if you missed a spot?* That may sound like a question about hygiene, but at its core it's about you: careless, reckless, dangerous.

Take driving. You hit a bump in the road. OCD asks: *What if that was a person?* Again, the surface is an event. But the hub is the same: negligent, oblivious guilty.

Take relationships. You don't feel affection in a particular moment. OCD whispers: *What if you don't really love them?* The theme looks like romance, but the accusation is deeper: loveless, defective, incapable of intimacy.

Take morality. You flinch at a violent news story and OCD twists it into: *What if you wanted that?* This isn't about the news. It's about branding you corrupt, tainted, untrustworthy.

Or on a depersonalized afternoon, OCD intones: *What if you're hollow, not real?* The theme looks existential, but the hub is unchanged: you are defective, incomplete, a fraud at your core.

And then there are subtler masks. An artist feels blocked, and OCD overlays the blank page with: *What if you're unoriginal, a fraud in disguise?*

A friend forgets to return a call, and OCD stages it as: *What if you're uncaring, incapable of real connection?*

A young professional struggles with a presentation and suddenly hears: *What if you're incompetent, an imposter who can't handle responsibility?*

Even personality traits can be conscripted. Being quiet becomes *You're aloof.* Being energetic becomes *You're overwhelming.* Having strong emotions becomes *You're unstable.*

The costumes vary, but the pattern is the same. Distrust what you sensed. Overlay imagination. Justify it with fragments ripped out of context. Promote it into "relevance." Stamp it with moral urgency.

By the time the mask lands, it doesn't look like theatre anymore. It looks like biography.

This is why so many people say: *It feels like my OCD keeps changing.* In reality, it isn't multiplying. It's orbiting.

The spoke may change, but the hub doesn't move. One person cycles through contamination, checking, harm, and relationship themes — yet underneath, the feared self is the same: *You are careless and dangerous.* Another rotates through morality, confession, and memory doubts — yet the feared self is steady: *You are corrupt.*

This is why the fears feel so personal. They're not random. They're tailored — custom-made to fit your deepest concerns.

OCD does not waste its costumes on identities you don't care about. It always performs under your brightest spotlight.

Selectivity of Doubt

If OCD were truly about uncertainty, you'd doubt everything.

You'd question every action, every choice, every detail of your day. But that's not what happens. A person who fears writing something wrong may re-read every email, line by line, yet never worry about whether they locked the door. Someone who checks the stove five times might never doubt the safety of their car.

Even in the thick of it, vast parts of life move untouched. You trust traffic lights, answer when your name is called, feel your coat on your shoulders and go.

That contrast is the tell. OCD doesn't carpet-bomb; it cherry-picks. It stages its show where the light's already warm — over the places your values live and your insecurities hum.

A new parent, aching to be good, can read ordinary tiredness as a moral signal. A first-year nurse who cares deeply about competence may treat a routine oversight like a character verdict. A partner hungry for closeness can misread a flat moment as proof of being loveless.

Not random. Targeted.

Watch how the pattern shows up first across themes. One person worries about papers left too close to a radiator but never about the cleanliness of their hands. Another fears Hepatitis C but not leaving the door unlocked. Someone drives back to scan a stretch of road for a body but never obsesses over germs. The themes rotate, but the identity accusation stays the same — careless, corrupt, defective, fraudulent.

If this were about real danger, the doubt would spread evenly. It doesn't. It clusters where your feared self would hurt most and leaves the rest of your life untouched.

And even within a single theme, the inconsistency continues. You might check the front door but not the back. Fear undercooked chicken but not room-temperature leftovers. You might picture one of your pets in danger again and again, yet never once imagine the same fate for the other.

If this were genuine reasoning, it would apply everywhere. The unevenness is the giveaway — obsessional logic isn't logic at all; it's stage lighting, bright where OCD wants you to look and dark everywhere else.

This selectivity is proof, not of the doubt, but against it.

If your memory were broken, it would fail everywhere. If your conscience were corrupt, it wouldn't flare only around the things you treasure. If your capacity to love were absent, you wouldn't care so much about the moments that feel flat.

The doubt sticks only where a counterfeit identity can be cast. Elsewhere, your reasoning is clear, your senses steady, your life unremarkably sane.

That same selectivity keeps reassurance fragile. When the illusion is anchored to the kind of person you're terrified of being, no amount of "low probability" talk will do. You're not arguing stats; you're warding off a mask.

So the mind keeps circling the same rooms: the email that "could have been off," the meeting where "something felt wrong," the memory with a missing frame.

The show plays there because the set is built there.

Once you see this, the spell thins. The doubt is not global. It isn't even consistent. It is local, strategic, and emotionally opportunistic.

It performs where a feared self would land the hardest and calls that "truth." But truth doesn't behave like that. Reality is boringly consistent.

Stop arguing with the content and look at the pattern.

The pattern shows irrelevance. If the same *what if* can be cast onto a harmless corner of your day and slide off without sticking, then its stickiness in one place is not evidence; it's staging.

And that takes us to the next move. The way out is not to win the argument in each selected room, nor to learn to suffer in them forever.

It's to expose the selection itself—and then apply the same five doorways you used on obsessional doubts to the feared self they serve.

Because the feared self isn't a hidden core that must be unearthed. It's just the show's headliner. The doorways will take it off the marquee.

Identity vs. Reality

At the core of the feared possible self lies its deadliest trick: the idea that imagination can reveal identity.

That a picture in your mind is a portrait of your soul. That a doctored memory is more reliable than your lived history. That a whispered line from OCD is somehow the truest line you've ever spoken.

But identity doesn't work that way. Who you are is not uncovered in imagination's theatre. Who you are is shown in the ordinary rhythm of your days.

The feared self is Photoshop, not mirror. It takes an image, distorts it, deepens the shadows, then holds it up and says: *Look, this is you.* You glance, recoil, and wonder. But no matter how convincing the edit, it is not the face you carry into the world.

The mirror shows your real life: the breakfast you made, the laugh you shared, the hand you held. Photoshop shows a mask composited from scraps and daubed in fear. It looks vivid, but it isn't real.

Or think of it as biography versus fanfiction. Your life is a book written in daily lines of ordinary care and effort. OCD barges in, seizes the manuscript, and starts writing pulp drama.

It invents scenes, twists motives, exaggerates flaws, casts you in roles you never played. The fanfiction feels lurid, gripping, unforgettable. That's why it feels heavier than your real story.

But it is not your story. It borrows your name and rewrites your plot.

Even the theatre itself obeys this law. A costume worn long enough feels like skin. A mask strapped tight feels welded to your face.

But when the curtain falls, the actor walks offstage unchanged. OCD insists the costume is permanent. Reality proves otherwise.

Every moment outside the bubble — eating, resting, showing up, caring — the mask slips. Beneath it, your life continues.

And this is the antidote to the feared self. Reality is not hidden somewhere deep inside, waiting for you to unearth it by endless analysis. It is already present — in the way you live when you're not dragged onto OCD's stage.

The clicked lock. The returned call. The child's laughter. The meal eaten. These are not clues pointing toward your identity. They *are* your identity.

OCD declares: *We've uncovered the truth of who you are.* Reality answers: *You've already shown who you are, every day you live.*

And that's why the next move isn't to argue the details of the costume. It's to walk the accusation itself through the same five doorways you used before — because a staged identity collapses the same way a staged danger does.

The Doorways Applied to the Feared Self

The feared self is not some disowned fragment of identity waiting to be integrated as in trauma work. It is a counterfeit role constructed entirely by OCD's stagecraft — a mask that only looks welded on until you see the wires. And because it's built with the same machinery as every other obsession, the same doorways dismantle it too.

Doorway 1: Imaginary.

The feared self is stitched from images, scenarios, and doctored memories. A picture of harm, a phantom confession, a false replay. All of it is imagination dressed as identity. Nothing in your direct, present experience confirms it.

Doorway 2: Irrelevant.

Even if imaginable, it doesn't belong in this moment. Cooking dinner, walking into work, holding your child — none of these scenes contain evidence of the feared self. The mask doesn't enter through reality. It barges in through misapplied relevance.

Doorway 3: Fundamentally False.

Every feared self is propped up by reasoning errors. Imagination treated as evidence. Possibility promoted into probability. Recoil misread as guilt. Distress mistaken for intent. Once you see the first false move, the whole verdict collapses.

Doorway 4: Not About Uncertainty.

This isn't a case of "learning to live with not knowing." It's recognizing a manufactured unknown. The feared self is not an unknowable truth. It is a counterfeit question. Asking you to tolerate uncertainty here is like asking you to live with not knowing if you're secretly two-dimensional. The premise itself is broken.

Doorway 5: Nothing to Resolve.

If the feared self is imaginary, irrelevant, false, and counterfeit, then what's left to fix? Nothing. The trial was never real. The mask was never skin. The moment you stop treating it as a case to be solved, the illusion begins to collapse.

The feared self only seems different because it targets your core. But the mechanics are the same. Which means the exits are the same too.

Key Insights

- The feared self is OCD's deepest illusion. It doesn't question doors or stoves — it questions you, fabricating a counterfeit identity that feels welded on.

- It is not discovered — it is manufactured. OCD stitches scraps of memory, imagination, and insecurity into masks and insists they reveal hidden truth.

- Values become weapons when hijacked. Love, honesty, morality, and responsibility are flipped into accusations, turning your compass into evidence against you.

- The feared self feels like revelation because OCD forges evidence. Doctored memories, phantom confessions, and cathedral echoes mimic gravity without offering truth.

- Selectivity exposes the illusion. OCD doubt doesn't spread everywhere; it only clusters where a counterfeit identity can hurt most, proving its irrelevance.

- Identity is shown in reality, not imagination. The life you live — meals made, hands held, work done — is your biography, not OCD's fanfiction.

- The same doorways dismantle the feared self. Imaginary, irrelevant, false, not true uncertainty, nothing to resolve — once you see these seams, the mask loosens.

- Compulsions exist only to escape the feared self. But there was never anything real to escape — the theatre goes dark the moment you stop cooperating with the show.

Try This: Unmask the Costume

This isn't about proving you're "good." It's about spotting a mask and stepping out of the scene.

1) Name the role.

Quietly label the costume that shows up (dangerous, corrupt, loveless, fraudulent, incompetent). Just the title, nothing more.

2) Call three witnesses from today.

List three plain facts from your day (a meal made, a message returned, a kindness shown). Not arguments—biography.

3) Notice the spotlight.

Ask: *Does this doubt appear everywhere—or only where it would hurt most?* Selectivity = staging, not truth.

4) Walk it through the five exits (one breath).

Imaginary? (built from images/"what ifs") → *Irrelevant?* (doesn't belong to this moment) → *False?* (reasoning stunt) → *Not real uncertainty?* (counterfeit problem) → *Nothing to resolve.*

5) Close the script.

Write one short line and stop:

- "This mask was stitched, not born."
- "My day already shows who I am."
- "There's nothing here to fix."

Then stop. No further debate. No reassurance. Just recognition. The feared self was never revelation. It was theatre. And the stage has gone dark.

No loitering in identity court.

Chapter 7

Living Beyond Obsessional Doubt

The End of the Show

Every show has to end. The stage lights dim, the actors bow, the audience files out. The theatre is designed to hold you spellbound, but the performance cannot run forever.

OCD is no different. It thrives on keeping you in your seat — repeating scenes, replaying lines, demanding one more round of applause. But there comes a point when you realize: you can walk out into the night air. The show will go on without you, but you are no longer part of the audience.

This is what living beyond obsessional doubt feels like. It's not about silencing imagination or dismantling every script. It's about leaving the theatre altogether. You don't wait for the curtain to fall. You simply stop buying tickets.

And when you walk out, you find yourself not in emptiness. You step into something more solid — call it *Original Experience.*

Original Experience is reality before OCD begins its performance. It's the door you just locked, the air you're breathing, the child you hug, the hand you hold. It isn't a thought about reality; it's reality itself.

The bubble lives off imagination. The feared self thrives on staged identities. But Original Experience is prior to both. It doesn't need defending, and it doesn't ask for proof. It just is.

Think of walking out of a dark cinema into the brightness of afternoon.

At first, your eyes ache. The light feels too strong, too bare. You want to retreat back into the shadows, where the story feels safer, more controlled. But after a moment, your eyes adjust. The daylight, once blinding, becomes steady, reliable, freeing.

Original Experience has that same quality. At first, it may feel almost too ordinary. No drama, no urgency, no verdicts. Just the steady hum of life as it is.

But that ordinariness is its strength. It is unmanufactured. It is not a mask. It doesn't need applause to exist.

And here is the most radical part: Original Experience is trustworthy. It doesn't demand cross-examination. It doesn't shift with imagination's tricks. You don't have to test it, check it, or rehearse it. You can rest in it.

You live it in small moments all the time. Drinking coffee in the morning — the taste, the warmth, the smell rising with the steam. Original Experience is there before the *what if* arrives.

Sitting in traffic — the hum of the engine, the pattern of brake lights, the rhythm of music in the background. Original

Experience holds you even when your mind is tempted to replay a phantom accident.

Hugging your child — the fabric of their shirt against your skin, the sound of their breath, the weight in your arms. Original Experience is there before the script tries to hand you a mask.

Or late at night, when the house is quiet. You lie down, feel the sheets against your skin, hear the faint tick of a clock. There's no revelation here, no identity on trial. Just being. Just reality.

This is why Original Experience can be described in almost spiritual terms. Not as a creed or doctrine, but as contact with something deeper — a directness that bypasses the bubble altogether. Reality as a gift, not as problem to be solved.

Original Experience is what OCD can never counterfeit. The theatre can imitate reality, it can mimic urgency, it can forge evidence. But it cannot generate the living texture of reality. That belongs to the world itself

Living beyond obsessional doubt means returning, again and again, to that given. To the air outside. To the ground under your feet. To the Original Experience of being here, now, without scripts.

Escape Velocity

Living beyond obsessional doubt isn't just about walking out of the theatre. It's about leaving orbit altogether — not just stepping outside the performance hall, but rising beyond its whole gravity well.

Think of OCD as a planet with its own gravity. For years, you lived entirely under its pull. Every thought curved back toward the bubble, every action was tugged by the compulsion to check, confess, or analyze. Even when you stepped away, you felt dragged back in.

But there is such a thing as escape velocity — the point where momentum carries you beyond the planet's pull. At first, you may still feel the echo tug, as if unseen hands were trying to reel you back. But with each refusal, each step into Original Experience, the pull weakens.

Until one day, you look back and the planet is shrinking — a blue marble in the dark, no longer dictating your path.This is what happens when you begin living more and more in Original Experience.

You don't need a single breakthrough or heroic launch. Freedom builds through small decisions: the door you don't recheck, the confession you don't make, the phantom danger you don't chase. Each act is fuel. Each choice tilts the balance. The spell thins, the pull fades, and life widens around you.

The old orbit no longer defines you. The bubble no longer contains you. The mask no longer fits.

Escape velocity doesn't mean you'll never again feel a flicker of OCD's gravity. It means that when it whispers, it no longer pulls you down. You've seen the illusion from above, and once seen, the strings are obvious. The show may keep advertising; the planet may still exist. But neither commands your flight.

You live now under a different gravity — the steady pull of Original Experience, the quiet trust of reality as it is. It doesn't clamor. It doesn't demand applause. Yet it holds you more firmly than obsessional doubt ever could. You don't have to cling to it. You're already inside it.

This is the freedom beyond obsessional doubt: not constant vigilance, not endless solving, not a life spent managing symptoms — but a change in orbit. A shift of gravity.

The planet may still exist, but it no longer holds you. You are carried forward by something truer, stronger, and infinitely more stable than illusion.

Living Without Solving

One of the hardest illusions to let go of is the belief that freedom comes from solving the doubt. That if you can just find the right answer, assemble enough proof, confess enough times, or argue convincingly with the mask, you'll finally be at peace.

But solving is the theatre's trick. Every attempt to solve inside imagination keeps you in your seat. Every time you chase an answer to *What if I'm corrupt?* or *What if I missed something?* you're buying another ticket.

The show continues because you keep participating. Living beyond obsessional doubt means stepping out of the game altogether. It means refusing the questions imagination throws like darts. Not managing its courtroom. Not tolerating its stage-urgency. Simply — not playing.

This doesn't mean abandoning reality. You still lock doors, pay bills, keep appointments, apologize when you've truly hurt someone. That's the work of ordinary living, and it rests on something solid: your Original Experience.

And here is the turn: certainty itself isn't the problem. Certainty is natural, and you already live by it every day. The trap is looking for it in imagination, where no answer ever holds. The certainty you long for is already present in your Original Experience — the direct, lived reality of what you see, hear, touch, and know in context. The sound of the latch closing. The texture of the steering wheel. The warmth of someone beside you. The ordinariness of daily life.

That is certainty enough. Everything else is theatre.

Think of a carnival game where the rings are rigged never to land on the bottles. You can keep throwing, over and over, convinced the next toss will be the one. Or you can drop the rings and walk away. The prizes were never real. The game was never winnable.

That's what solving in imagination is like: you keep tossing, waiting for the satisfying "clink" of certainty, but it never comes. Meanwhile, Original Experience has already given you what you need — the sound of the bolt sliding home, the weight of the steering wheel, the warmth of a hug, the continuity of your lived history.

These are the anchors. These are the ground.

At first, walking away feels reckless. You're used to rehearsing the script, scanning for danger, demanding guarantees. To do nothing feels irresponsible, even dangerous. But that urgency is the illusion itself. Reality does not beg for constant analysis. Reality is already settled in your hands, your senses, your life.

You don't solve whether you love your child; you live it in hugs, meals, and bedtime stories. You don't solve whether you're honest; you live it in your words and choices. And once you taste that difference, the demand to solve loses its grip.

You recognize the carnival for what it was: just a noisy trick, built to keep you playing. You see it for what it is: another ticket seller, another script, another way of holding you in the bubble.

Freedom isn't about solving doubts in imagination. Freedom is trusting what's already in your hands — the ground beneath your feet, the life that's happening now.

Everyday Anchors

When you stop solving, the world doesn't vanish. And in its going, it steadies you. Life itself becomes the anchor.

You don't have to invent techniques or rituals to stay free. Everyday moments, once stripped of OCD's script, hold you steady without effort. The anchors were always there — you just didn't recognize them because OCD trained you to look past them, searching for a louder certainty.

Take conversation.

When you're speaking with a friend, OCD may try to pull you inward — *Did I say the wrong thing? Did I lie? Did I sound strange?*

But if you let go of the script, you notice what's already happening: two voices, words exchanged, laughter shared. Conversation is its own anchor. You don't need to solve it. The fact of it is enough.

Or food. You sit down to eat. The taste, the texture, the rhythm of chewing and swallowing. Ordinary, unremarkable — yet this is life itself. You're not proving anything, not answering any doubt. You're simply eating dinner.

Reality nourishes without asking for a verdict.

Or work. You reply to an email, attend a meeting, solve a practical problem. OCD whispers: *But what if you overlooked something? What if you're incompetent?*

But the reality is in front of you: tasks completed, coworkers responding, projects moving. Work itself is an anchor — a flow of reality that holds you without theatre.

The office hum, the small victories, the steady rhythm of tasks — they tether you to the real without effort.

Or play. You kick a ball in the yard, watch a film, play a game. For a moment, OCD tries to interrupt: *Shouldn't you be checking? Shouldn't you be rehearsing?*

But the ball is still rolling, the movie is still playing, the game is still unfolding.

Play anchors you in the real. Joy doesn't need defending. It happens in the doing.

Even rest. You lie down, the bed supporting your weight, the quiet of night settling around you. OCD may press: *What if you forgot something? What if you should get up?*

But rest itself is the anchor. The sheet against your skin, the rhythm of your breath, the continuity of sleep waiting to come. The stillness is its own proof — nothing is missing.

None of these are dramatic. That is their strength. They don't need to shout. They don't need to prove themselves. They don't demand applause. They simply hold you, the way gravity holds you to the earth.

This is the paradox: The anchors that free you from OCD are the same things you once overlooked as irrelevant. The hug, the meal, the conversation, the workday. Nothing mystical. Nothing extraordinary. Just reality, lived without a script.

Everyday life reveals itself as enough. It was always enough. And not just enough — it reveals itself as solid, steady, more trustworthy than any script could ever be.

What OCD once dismissed as too plain, too ordinary, too "not enough" is in fact the ground you've been searching for all along.

Hope and Continuity

When you first see through obsessional doubt, it can feel fragile — like the illusion might return at any moment. But fragility is part of the trick. The truth is, once the wires are exposed, the spell never has the same power again.

The bubble isn't something you carry forever. It isn't part of your nature. It's a trick — and once you recognize the trick, it loses its authority.

You may still notice the posters, hear the echoes, catch glimpses of the mask. But you no longer believe it's the truth. You see it for what it is: theatre.

This is not the same as saying doubt will vanish forever. The illusionist may still clear his throat, raise the curtain, and try to run the old routine. But this time you see it differently. What once felt gripping now looks flimsy, even clumsy — lines from a play you've outgrown.

Original Experience is what remains. Solid, trustworthy, ordinary. It doesn't need defending, and it doesn't need rehearsal. The more you live in it, the less the theatre even registers. The bubble is burst not because you outargue it, but because you no longer mistake it for reality.

Hope, then, is not learning to endure endless doubts. It's just the encore: the same old illusionist hoping you'll lean in for one more gasp. But you've already walked out. You know the trick. That's enough.

And when doubts resurface — as they sometimes will — don't panic. It isn't relapse. It's just the encore act of the same old illusionist, fishing for applause. But you've already left the theatre. You've seen the trick. You don't have to sit down again.

This is the freedom Original Experience offers: not coping, not managing, not tolerating, but seeing through. Once seen, the illusion dissolves. Once dissolved, reality holds.

The theatre may still exist, but it cannot command you. The show was never mandatory. Reality was always waiting outside.

And once you know the way back, the door never closes.

A Last Word

If you take only one thing from this book, let it be this: Doubt was never the truth.

It was an illusion, staged by imagination, sold as urgent, and mistaken for reality. You don't have to fight it, fix it, or solve it. You only have to see it. And once seen, the illusion cannot command you.

What remains is Original Experience — the ground beneath your feet, the breath in your chest, the life you're already living. This was never fragile, never absent. It was always here, waiting outside the theatre.

So go live. Not perfectly, not dramatically. But ordinarily. Eat the meal, walk the street, love the people around you. The show was never mandatory. Reality was always enough.

And remember this:

Once you've seen behind the curtain, the magician can't fool you the same way again.

You may still hear the patter, catch the echo of a script, glimpse the wires — but that's all they are now. Wires. Props. Tricks.

What matters is perspective.

The illusion is broken, and life is yours again.

Need More Help?

If you've reached the end and still feel tangled in doubt — that's not failure. That's why this page exists.

The Doubt Illusion was meant to make obsessional doubt understandable, approachable, and beatable. But for some, the illusion is more entrenched. When you've rehearsed these patterns for years, even seeing the trick may not stop the reflex to react.

You're not broken or "too complicated." You're simply facing a more elaborate illusion — one that needs more than a pocket guide to unwind.

That's what the *Resolving OCD Series* is for — the official two-volume guide and workbook grounded in Inference-Based Cognitive Behavioral Therapy (ICBT). Instead of just shining a flashlight on the illusion, it walks you through its architecture — step by step, layer by layer — with in-depth exercises and guided examples to help you dismantle it completely.

If *The Doubt Illusion* is a lens, the *Resolving OCD series* is the full blueprint — not "better," just more comprehensive when you need it.

You can also find free resources and ICBT-informed professionals at www.icbt.online — a site offering articles, practical tools, and a directory of therapists familiar with this approach.

If your distress is severe or life-limiting, please consider working with a licensed mental health professional experienced in ICBT. Sometimes the illusion runs deeper. That's okay. It just means a longer script — and a few more stage cues — before the curtain falls.

The show still ends.

About The Author

Dr. Frederick Aardema is a clinical psychologist, researcher, and professor in the Department of Psychiatry and Addiction at the University of Montreal. For nearly three decades, he has dedicated his career to understanding and treating obsessive-compulsive disorder (OCD), with a focus on how doubt, imagination, and self-perceptions fuel the problem.

He is the co-creator of Inference-Based Cognitive Behavioral Therapy (I-CBT), an evidence-based approach that helps people recognize how obsessional doubts are constructed — and how they dissolve once seen for what they are. His research, clinical work, and writing have helped shape a new way of understanding OCD, one that empowers people to step outside the illusion of doubt and reconnect with reality as it is.

Frederick is the author of several books on OCD and its treatment, including the acclaimed *Resolving OCD* series, which has given hope and clarity to readers and clinicians worldwide. He is also the director of the OCD Clinical Study Center at the Montreal Mental Health University Institute Research Center, where he leads clinical trials to improve treatment outcomes for those with OCD. His work has been widely published, presented internationally.

Outside of research and clinical work, Frederick enjoys time with his family, gardening, and cooking — ordinary experiences that remind him daily of the freedom and joy found in simple things. And most recently, he has been developing a taste for fine Scottish whisky, a pursuit he justifies as "cross-cultural research."

www.ingramcontent.com/pod-product-compliance
Lightning Source LLC
Chambersburg PA
CBHW070333090426
42733CB00012B/2459